Learn Sailing Right!
Beginning Sailing

The National Standard for Quality Sailing Instruction

The Small Boat Certification Series

In memory of Quentin McGown

Published by the UNITED STATES SAILING ASSOCIATION.

ISBN 978-0-9794677-2-1.
Printed in the United States of America.

UNITED STATES SAILING ASSOCIATION
P.O. BOX 1260, 15 MARITIME DRIVE, PORTSMOUTH, RI 02871-6015

Cover photograph by David Grossman, www.gurnetroad.com

Acknowledgements

Sailors can be wonderful people. Their love of the sport and their willingness to contribute time and effort for the good of fellow sailors is remarkable. That commitment and dedication to purpose has been present in every phase of the creation of Learn Sailing Right! Beginning Sailing.

Many people have been involved in the development of Learn Sailing Right! Beginning Sailing, the first book in the Learn Sailing Right! series. But, we must recognize those that created the foundation on which Learn Sailing Right! Beginning Sailing is built, the progenitors of Start Sailing Right! The family of US SAILING Small Boat Sailing instructional materials owes a life-long debt to Timmy Larr, Derrick Fries, Susie Trotman, Mark Smith, Jim Muldoon, and the National Faculty members of years past. Due to the efforts of these individuals, we continue to create the premier educational materials in sailing today.

Rich Jepsen, Training Division Chairman, is owed a debt of gratitude for sharing in the vision of this series and providing the leadership to create the best training materials available. Special appreciation is given to Janine Connelly, US SAILING's Training Director, and her staff for keeping this project on track and making the unwieldy manageable.

Project management Sheila McCurdy, US SAILING's National Faculty chair, vice commodore of the Cruising Club of America and U.S. Naval Academy Fales Committee member, supervised this project from the start. From drafting a business plan and coordinating initial efforts with illustration and design, to directing teams of volunteers, she guided Learn Sailing Right from the concept stage.

Hart Kelley, US SAILING's Associate Training Director, National Faculty member and Small Boat Master Instructor Trainer, and Kim Hapgood, Program Director of Sail Newport and National Faculty member and Small Boat Master Instructor Trainer, took us from fifty-percent to publication. Final editing, illustration changes and design coordination were all due to their diligence and tenacity.

Writing The initial concept of Learn Sailing Right! was drafted by John Kantor, founder and Director of Longshore Sailing School. Sheila McCurdy, working with US SAILING's National Faculty, turned that early vision into the book we have today.

Editing Andy German, publications department editor at Mystic Seaport, brought a keen eye and efficacious contributions to Learn Sailing Right!

Illustration Our many thanks to illustrator, surfer, and sailor Michael Boardman for turning difficult concepts into facile visuals.

Design Our thanks to graphic designer Darcy Magratten, whose talents assembled our work into greater coherence.

Content consulting To our field of experts, the National Faculty members Kim Hapgood, Hart Kelley, Morgan Collins, Derrick Fries, Rachel Miller, Peter Durant, Betsy Alison, John Kantor, Jo Mogle, Rich Brew, Guy Fleming, Alex Howland, and Sarah Kent we express our appreciation for their insights, contributions, edits, dedication and volunteerism.

Dan Nerney

As I come up on deck for the first day of a week long cruise, I'm greeted by the best question that can be asked in sailing, "would you like to take the helm?" "I'm ready", was my quick reply.

With my hands on the wheel, my feet planted on the deck, and with anticipation running high, I steered the boat away from the wind. As the sails filled, the boat heeled and we were underway. This is a magic moment that always makes me feel good. The sky, clouds, sails, boat, water, wind and my body all seemed to exist as one. And best of all, this feeling happens on every boat of any size.

Freedom, the connection with the sea, the passion for enjoying life, your mates are just a few of the reasons to spend time on the water. Boats come alive under sail and invigorate crews.

For the first time aspirant sailing might seem intimidating, but thanks to *Learn Sailing Right!*, one can quickly understand the concepts thanks to simple diagrams and clear descriptions. This book gets right to the basics and serves as a practical guide and handy reference for the entire crew.

Time on the water is precious. For many, sailing is the icing on the cake of life. Take some time to study this concise book on sailing and soon, you too will be happy to take the helm, embracing an opportunity that will last a lifetime.

Gary Jobson

Contents

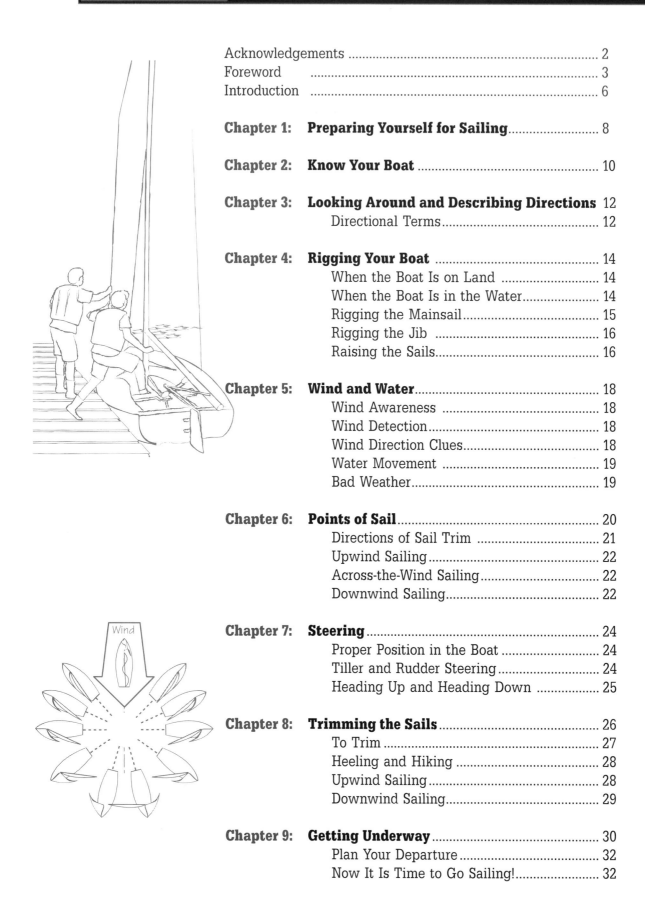

US SAILING's training programs are designed to help you join the ranks of the hundreds of thousands of adults and youths who have learned to sail on the lakes, rivers, bays and coasts of the United States. US SAILING is the National Governing Body of Sailing. Instructors certified by US SAILING work for the best sailing schools and programs in the country. We make learning to sail safe and fun for all ages.

This and the other books in the Small Boat Certification Series are professionally designed to present the information you need to get the most out of sailing. The series will be a convenient reference before and after your times on the water.

Like all new pursuits, sailing has its own set of skills and maneuvers that need to be learned and practiced. This book teaches you how to feel comfortable as skipper or crew and gives you a basic understanding of

nautical terms. The first part of the book gives you a "tour" of a typical small sailboat. The next section shows the concepts of how a boat moves through the water using the wind as "fuel." The middle section puts you on board the boat and describes how to steer and trim the sails to go where you want to go. The book wraps up with seamanship skills that make sailing safer and easier.

Sailing can bring you relaxing days on the water, adventurous family fun or challenging competition. You will be able to choose how you want to enjoy recreational sailing as you practice and gain experience. With this book you will learn the skills to build your confidence and ability to sail. Experienced instruction and use of this book will improve the pace you learn to sail.

Fair winds and good fun!

Sailors like to apply the Scouts' motto, "***Be prepared***," when they sail, and it certainly applies to clothing because the weather and sailing conditions can change quickly.

Sailing can give you a wonderful sense of freedom out on the water in the bright sun and cooling breeze. Even if you are new to sailing, you should recognize that overexposure—like sunburn and getting cold or wet—can reduce the fun and safety of sailing.

You can be away from land for hours at a time, so you need to dress for the local weather and bring only what you need. The air temperature on the water may be significantly different than on shore. Dress in comfortable clothes that allow you to move easily, wear shoes with nonskid soles, and bring a jacket or raingear that is water and wind resistant. Layering clothing helps you adjust to changes in temperature and wind conditions. Bring a waterproof bag for extra clothing and your personal items.

CHECKLIST:

Be Prepared

For sun protection:
- Sun glasses and a hat with a brim
- Sunscreen and lip balm: SPF 15 or higher
- Long-sleeve lightweight shirt and long pants

For warm and possibly wet conditions:
- Light-colored, breathable, quick-drying clothing
- Waterproof bag for clothing, wallet, cellphone, etc.

For cool or wet weather:
- Layers of lightweight clothing that dry quickly
- Jacket that sheds rain or spray
- Waterproof bag for clothing, wallet, cellphone etc.

For boat and water safety:
- PFD (personal flotation device or life jacket)
- Rubber-soled shoes (sneakers) that cover your toes
- Gloves to protect your hands
- Water bottle to keep hydrated

You should wear a PFD (personal flotation device), also known as a life jacket, even if you are a good swimmer because:

- You may be holding a boat off of a beach (see page 30-32).
- You could fall overboard (see page 58).
- The boat may tip over (see page 56-57).
- You may be better able to help others in the water.

Choose a proper life jacket:

- U. S. Coast Guard approved: The jacket should have an official label indicating the type of PFD and proper weight range of the wearer.
- Proper size and fit: Adjust the straps for a snug fit to keep the jacket from riding up when you are floating in the water.
- Bright color: Yellow is easier to see in the water.
- Good condition: No tears, broken zippers or damaged straps.

The U.S. Coast Guard requires that a PFD for each person be on board. Local regulations may require wearing a PFD. Learn what the laws are in your area.

A great variety of sailboats exist to suit every type of sailor, from eight-foot prams sailed by children, to huge, fast, ocean multihulls with professional crews. Stable daysailers are suitable for family outings, and high-performance dinghies thrill competitive athletes. Yet all sailboats share the same basic elements: Hull, Fins, Rigging, Spars and Sails.

Within these basic elements are many parts with specific names to help sailors communicate.

The hull is the body of the boat to which every-thing else is attached. Multihulls have more than one hull: catamarans have two and trimarans have three hulls. Most learn-to-sail boats are monohulls with one hull.

The front of any hull is called the bow, and the back is the stern. The cockpit is the interior where people usually sit. The outside surface of the hull below the water is called the bottom.

The fins are "appendages" of the hull. The rudder is attached to the stern and connects to the tiller that is used for steering. The "board" helps prevent the hull from sideslipping through the water and is the pivot point around which the boat turns. A boat has one of the following:

- Centerboard, which swings up and down in the center of the boat inside a structure called a trunk.
- Daggerboard, which is pushed and pulled almost straight up and down in a trunk.
- Leeboard, which swings like a centerboard, but is attached to the side of the hull.
- Keel, which is fixed to the hull and cannot be raised.

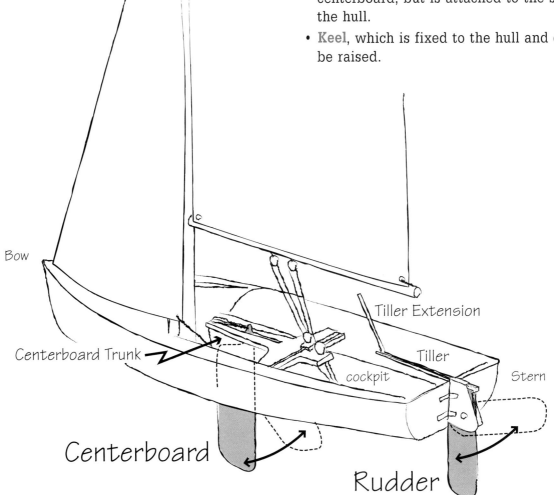

Bow

Tiller Extension

Centerboard Trunk

Tiller

cockpit

Stern

Centerboard

Rudder

Sails are wing-shaped to use the wind to propel the boat. Most sails are triangular:

- The **head** is the top corner.
- The **luff** is the front edge of the sail.
- The **tack** is the corner between the luff and foot.
- The **foot** is the bottom side.
- The **clew** is the corner between the leech and foot.
- The **leech** is the back edge.
- The leech has stiffeners called **battens**.

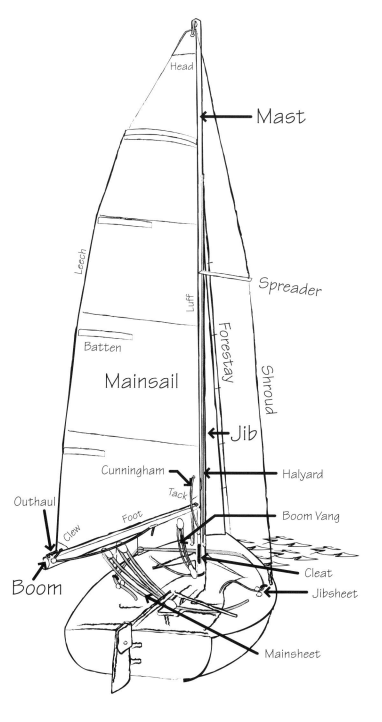

The **spars** spread the sails. The **mast** is the vertical spar. The **boom** attaches to the mast at a right angle to hold the bottom of the mainsail.

Rigging is divided into two groups depending on how it is used.

Standing rigging is wire used to help the mast stand upright:

- **Stays** hold the mast from going forward and back.
- **Shrouds** keep the mast from falling sideways.

Running rigging is the **line** (rope) used for adjusting the sails:

- **Halyards** are used to raise and lower the sails.
- **Sheets** move the sails in and out.
- The **outhaul** stretches the foot of the sail along the boom.
- The **cunningham** stretches the luff.
- The **boom vang** prevents the boom from rising.
- Running rigging is secured to **cleats**.

While there is a lot to learn on board a boat, you also need to be aware of what is going on around you on the water. Keep an eye on where you started from so you can sail back. Learn to recognize tide and current by their effects on docks and floats. Watch and listen for other boats approaching and be sure to keep a safe distance. No matter what is happening on the boat, always keep an eye out for what is going on around you.

Directional Terms

Just as parts of the boat have specific names, a sailor needs terms to describe things relative to the boat. Directional terms help you locate something onboard or describe where to look for something of interest on the water or shore. The first thing to learn is that when facing forward the left side of the boat is the **port** side and the right side is the **starboard**.

Keeping a Weather Eye

- Watch the clouds for weather changes.
- Track boats around you to avoid collisions.
- Be aware of the current's affect on your progress.
- Watch water depth to avoid hitting bottom.
- Keep track of where "home" is.

You have learned that the front of the boat is the bow, and the back of the boat is the stern. The direction toward the bow is **forward**. Beyond the bow, you would see something **ahead**. Toward the stern is **aft**. Beyond the stern is **astern**.

The area about halfway between the bow and stern is the **midships**. Halfway between the sides of the boat anywhere from bow to stern is on the **centerline**. Something that is beyond either side of the boat at right angles (90°) to the centerline is considered **abeam**.

Knowing where the wind is coming from relative to the boat is always essential. **Windward** is the side from which the wind blows. The opposite side is **leeward** (pronounced "lou-ward"). The wind direction is referred to geographically as well. For example, a north wind blows from the north and a southwest wind from the southwest.

When the wind is coming from the port side (with the sails to starboard), a sailboat is said to be on **port tack**. When the wind is coming from the starboard side (with the sails to port), a sailboat is said to be on **starboard tack.**

Port and **Starboard**: To help you distinguish port from starboard, remember port and left each have four letters.

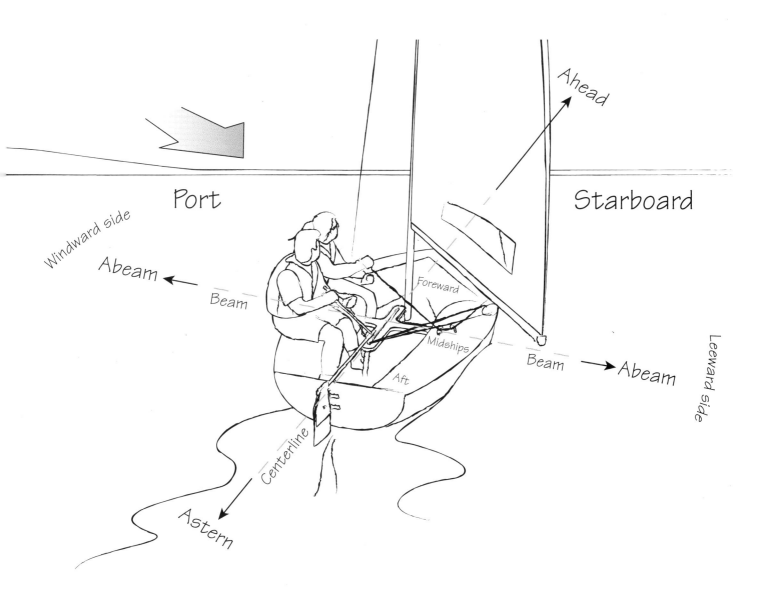

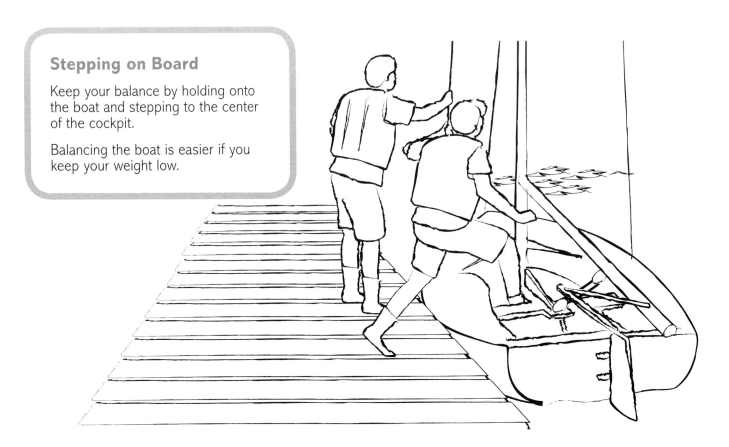

Stepping on Board

Keep your balance by holding onto the boat and stepping to the center of the cockpit.

Balancing the boat is easier if you keep your weight low.

Rigging-up is a chance to get your hands on the boat and put to use what you have learned. Look over the boat to make sure you understand how things are to be connected and fastened correctly when the time comes. Boats can vary, but here are the general steps for getting a boat ready to sail.

When the Boat is on Land

Don't step into the boat when the bottom is on land or supports; otherwise you could damage the hull. Instead, reach in over the sides to rig the mainsail and jib. You can hang the **rudder** on its fittings only if it is designed to pivot up into a shallow position for launching.

Make sure to insert all **drain plugs** into the holes that allow rain water to run out when the boat is stored. If you forget, the cockpit will flood when sailing.

When the Boat is in the Water

Make sure the boat is secured to the dock with the bow line. Step into the boat near the centerline of the cockpit. At the same time, hold on to a part of the boat like the mast to steady yourself and move into the boat without hesitation. If you put your weight on the side of the boat, it could tip more than you expect, and you could fall into the water. Lower the centerboard or daggerboard and adjust your weight to stabilize the boat before another crew steps into the middle of the boat. Check to see that the rudder and tiller are in place.

Rigging the Mainsail

The mainsail may be folded like an accordion or rolled like a tube. Begin by attaching the foot. The foot should be on the outside of the roll or the long side of the accordion fold.

The clew goes to the aft end of the boom. The foot may or may not be attached to the boom depending on the rig type. If the boom has a groove, you will need to slide the foot of the sail into it while pulling the clew aft. Once the foot has been fed into the groove on the boom, attach the tack.

The tack – usually where the sailmaker's logo is – attaches to the forward end of the boom. Next, attach the outhaul to the clew. Make sure the sail stays untwisted by running your hands along the sides of the leech or the luff as you prepare to raise the sail up the mast. The head, the narrowest corner, attaches to the main halyard. Look up the mast to be sure the halyard is not wrapped around anything. Keep some tension on the main halyard while you start hoisting the luff several inches up the mast. Secure the end of the halyard to keep the luff from falling out of the mast groove. With the sail partially rigged, check to make sure the battens are in place along the leech. If not, insert them.

Six Rigging Steps for the Mainsail

1. Unroll the sail.

2. Feed the foot into the groove in the boom, clew corner first.

3. Attach the tack, then the clew, and finish with the head.

4. Check for battens.

5. Loosen the mainsheet and boomvang.

5. Raise the sail up the mast 6-12 inches and secure until you are ready to raise the sails and go sailing.

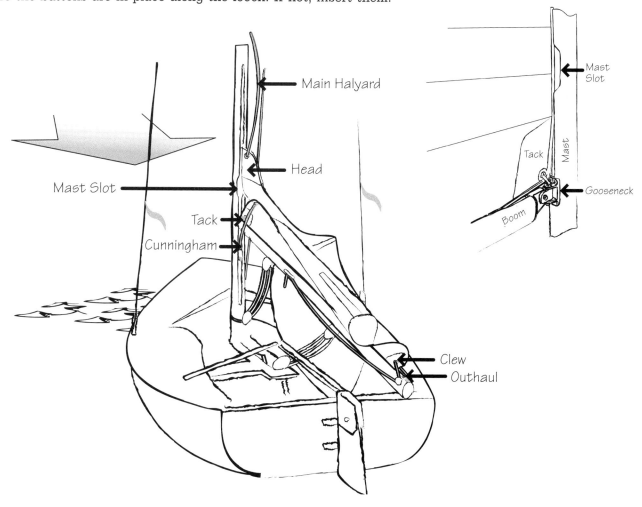

Rigging the Jib

First, attach the tack of the sail near the bottom of the forestay. If the sail has jib hanks, snaps or clips, attach them to the forestay from the tack up to the head making sure the sail is not twisted. Attach the jib halyard to the head. Be sure the halyard can run clear without any tangles in the rigging above. More often than not, jibs are stored with sheets already attached. If you need to attach your sheets, find the middle of the line you will use and attach it to the jib with a cow hitch knot (see page 51). Then, run the free ends of the jibsheets through the jib fairleads on each side of the cockpit. Tie a figure-eight stopper knot (see page 51) in the end of each sheet so it can't pull back through the jib fairlead.

Raising the Sails

Before pulling up the halyards, ease out the sheets and boom vang so the sails will luff – flutter in the wind – and the boom is free to move while you are raising the sail. Check that the centerboard and rudder are down as far as they can go without hitting the bottom. Alert everyone on the boat to be aware of the boom which may swing from side-to-side as the mainsail is raised. Raise the jib first, then the mainsail.

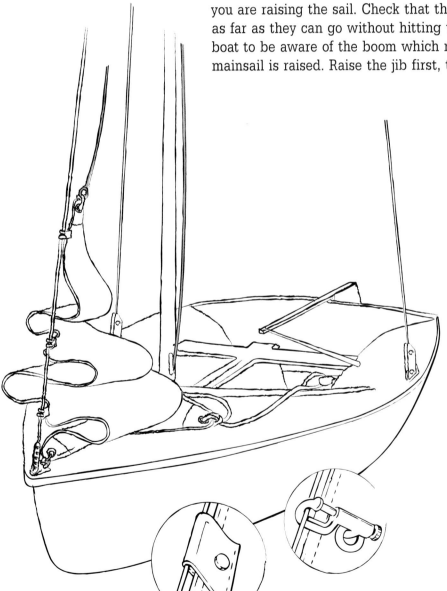

Five Rigging Steps for the Jib

1. Unroll the jib.

2. Attach tack.

3. Clip on hanks.

4. Attach halyard to the head.

5. Lead sheets through fairleads.

Raise the jib until:
- the luff is taut;
- the wrinkles have smoothed out.

Cleat and coil (see page 51) the halyard.

Let the jib luff while you raise the mainsail.

Raise the mainsail until:
- the head is at the top of the mast;
- the luff wrinkles have disappeared;
- the boom is parallel to the water.

Cleat and coil the halyard.

Let the mainsail luff.

Allow the boom to swing freely and avoid getting hit by it.

Tighten the outhaul, cunningham and boomvang.

> Position the bow into the wind when raising sails so the sails do not fill with wind.

> When coiling a halyard for storage while sailing, be sure that you do not wrap or crown the coil (as seen on page 51). Instead, wedge the coils between the halyard and mast. This way, if you need to lower the sail quickly the halyard will run freely.

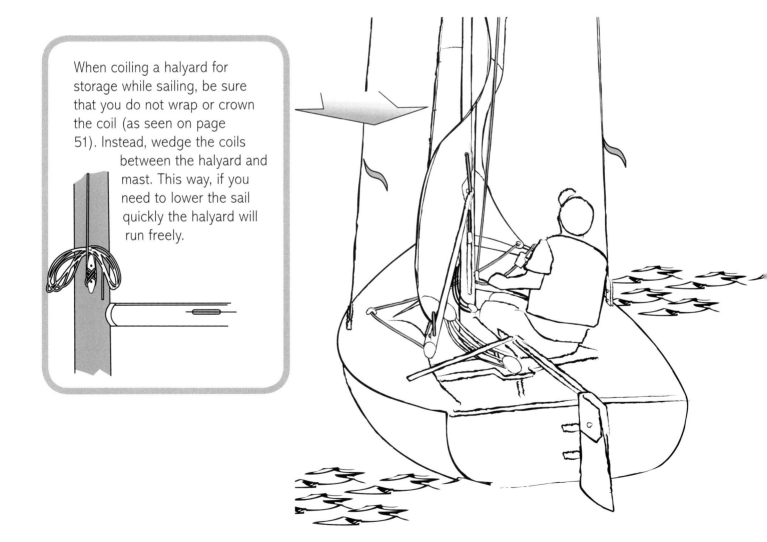

Wind Awareness

The next chapter gives many ways to "see" the wind when you are out on the water. When preparing to sail, you need to know the wind direction to make raising the sails easier. Look around. You might see a flag waving from a pole, or the telltale, a piece of yarn tied to the shroud, streaming in the breeze. Position your boat so the bow points into the wind.

Sailing needs wind and water. Wind on the sails can push – and even pull – the hull through the water. The wind direction determines how to position the sails to keep the boat moving forward. Sailors should know where the wind is coming from and the wind angle relative to their boat for sail-trim purposes (Chapter 8). Gentle, steady breezes (5-10 mph) and little or no current in the water are ideal for learning to sail.

Wind Detection

The speed and direction of the wind are often variable. Wind is occasionally very strong and sometimes calm. Even a modest breeze may have ups and downs in wind speed. Brief increases in velocity are known as puffs, while decreases are lulls. Wind direction can shift dramatically over hours or just slightly every few minutes. With practice, you will learn to "see" changes in the wind's direction and strength.

> When checking wind direction, use stationary flags. If a boat is moving, the speed of the boat affects the way its onboard flags are flying.

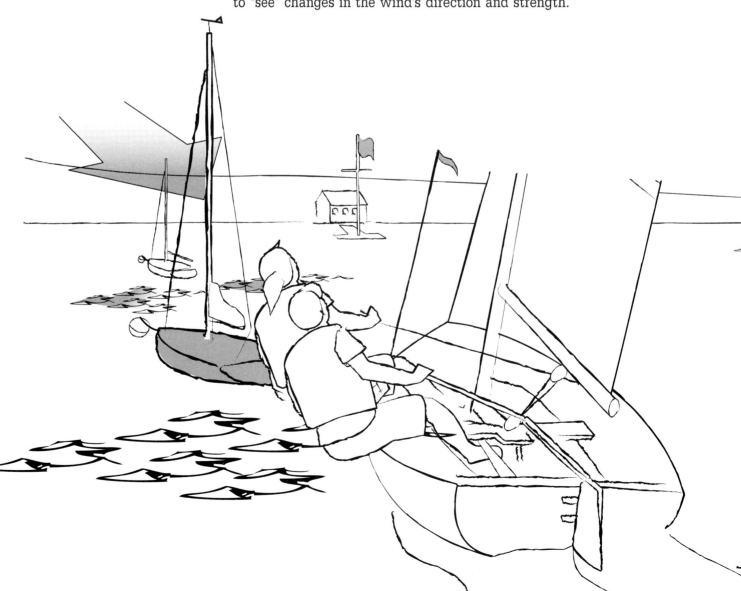

Wind Direction Clues

1. Look at the trimtales on the shrouds of your boat.

2. Look at the ripples on the water. The wind creates rows of wavelets at right angles to its direction. Calm glassy areas with few ripples characterize lulls, and darker, spiky ripples show areas of puffs.

3. Feel the wind on your face, neck or hands.

4. Notice how boats at anchor usually face into the wind, unless they also have current pushing them.

5. Look on shore for flags and smokestacks.

Water Movement

Water movement is affected by many things, including the earth's gravitational pull and wind force. In bodies of water open to the ocean, the rise and fall of water on a predictable schedule is called tide. The horizontal flow of water is called current. Sometimes current moves faster than a boat can sail!

The range of tide – the depth difference between high and low water – is important because you might run aground in a place where you had enough water just a few hours before. Boats pulled up on a beach at low tide could float away at high tide.

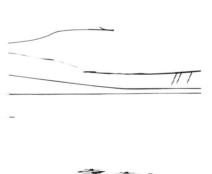

To see if the tide changed, look at objects along the shore. Is the top of the pier higher above the water surface than before? Is more beach exposed to view? Is the ramp to the floating dock more level than before? Look for signs of current by examining an anchored float or buoy to see if it has a little wake trailing from it. This indicates the direction in which the current is flowing. You can find information on tides for the dates when you plan to be on the water from Web sites, newspapers, news broadcasts, weather radios and tide tables available at bookstores and marine stores.

Bad weather

Good sailors are alert to changes in the weather that could signal the onset of inclement conditions for sailing. Recognizing the early warnings for high winds or storms can give you time to reduce sail or seek shelter. Watch the distant sky for signs of change and listen to a weather radio for local forecasts. "When in doubt, don't go out!"

Remember that it takes longer to sail against the current. If possible, it is a good idea to sail "up current" first so the current can help bring you back to your starting point, even if the wind dies.

Since wind and weather are constantly changing, it is a good idea to keep a "weather eye" looking for signs of change.

Once you know the wind direction, you can trim the sails for the direction you want to go. In the simplest form of sailing, a boat and its sails can be pushed "downwind," with the wind coming over the stern. But keep in mind that if you sail downwind, you will need to work your way back upwind to return to your starting place.

For 270° of the wind circle you can match the correct sail position to the wind – sails are pulled in tighter for sailing upwind and let out farther for sailing downwind. The **No-Go Zone** is roughly a 90° area that is too close to the wind to sail in effectively, but it is possible to sail on either side of the zone and zigzag your way to windward (see chapter 12). Sailors can reach destinations in all directions.

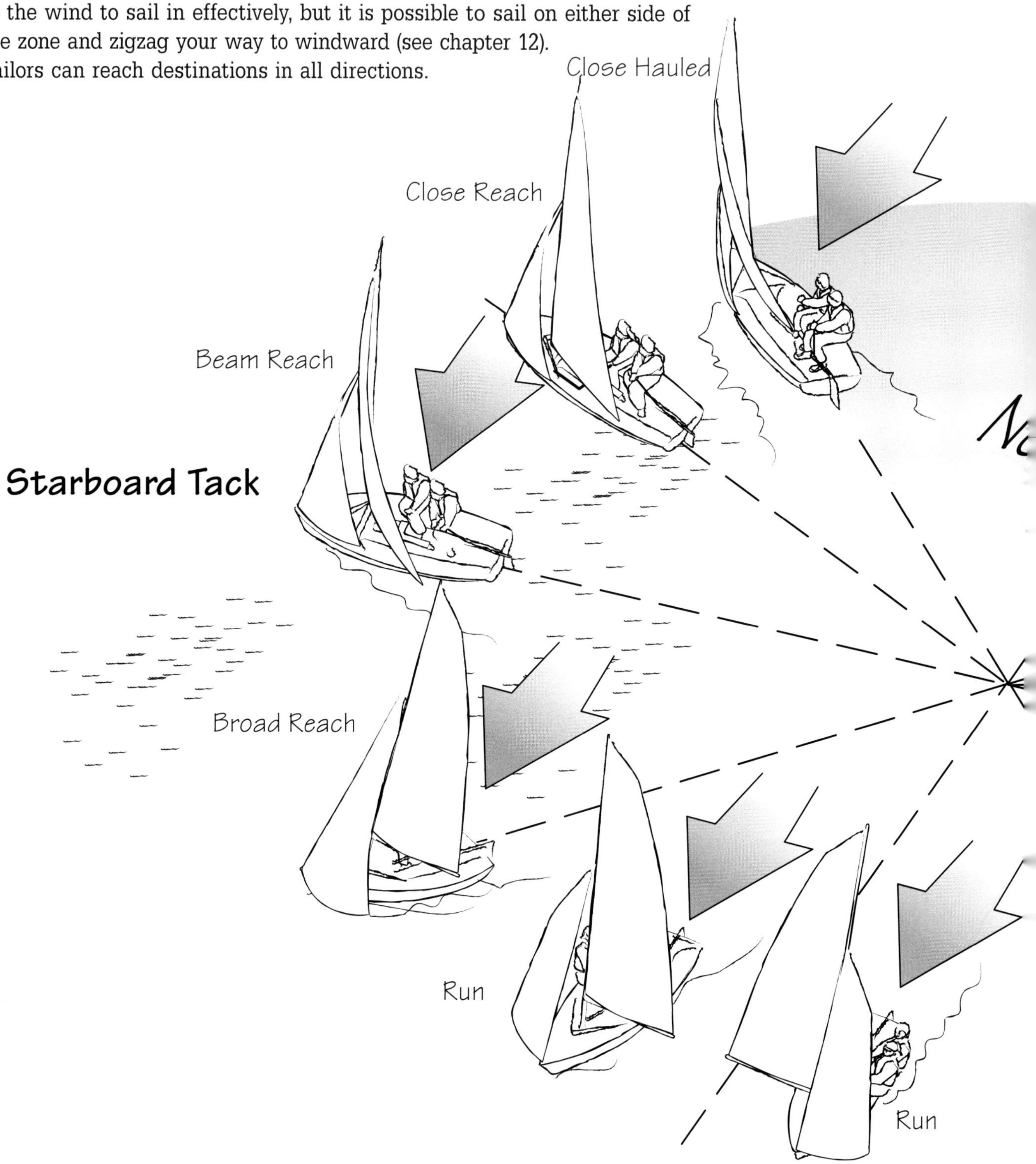

Close Hauled

Close Reach

Beam Reach

Starboard Tack

Broad Reach

Run

Run

Directions of Sail Trim

Sailors divide the wind circle into six sections, one being the No-Go zone. The others are the five points of sail.

Upwind sailing is sailing toward the direction from which the wind is blowing. It includes two points of sail: **Close-Hauled** and **Close Reaching**.

Sailing across the wind is called **Beam Reaching**.

Downwind sailing refers to sailing in the direction to which the wind is blowing. It includes both **Broad Reaching** and **Running**.

The same five points of sail apply whether the wind is coming over the port or the starboard side.

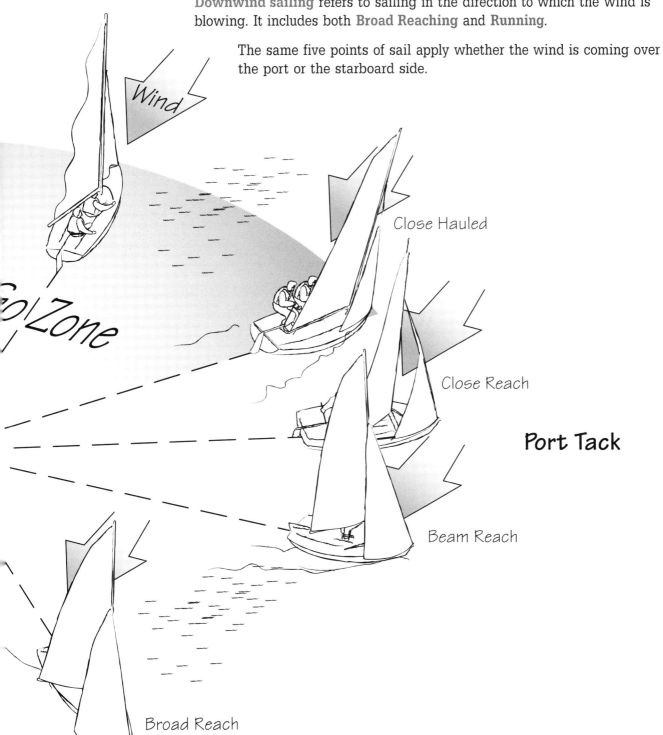

Wind

Go Zone

Close Hauled

Close Reach

Port Tack

Beam Reach

Broad Reach

The safety position allows you to take a break from active sailing in a safe, controlled manner. Steer to a close reach and ease the sheets, allowing the sails to luff completely. With all the wind spilled out of the sails, the boat will glide to a stop and give you a break from the action. When you are ready to sail again, pull in the sails to start moving. When in the safety position, keep the boat on a close reach.

A close reach is best for the safety position.

When close-hauled the swinging boom might bump your head as the mainsail luffs.

On a broad reach or run, the sails will not luff enough to stop the boat. Turn toward the wind until the sails luff completely.

The details of sail trim are covered in Chapter 8, but here are the six sections of the sailing "pie":

1. No-Go Zone: A boat cannot sail in the No-Go Zone. It is the area 45° to either side of the wind direction where sails always luff and the boat slows to a stop.

Upwind Sailing

2. Close-Hauled: The boat is about 45° from the wind direction. The sails are trimmed in close, with the boom positioned somewhere between the centerline and the leeward side of the hull.

3. Close Reach: The boat is sailing about 60° to 75° from the wind direction. The sails are let out just on the verge of luffing.

Across-the-Wind Sailing

4. Beam Reach: The boat is sailing approximately 90° or perpendicular to the wind – the wind is abeam. The sails are let out about halfway, just on the verge of luffing.

Downwind Sailing

5. Broad Reach: The boat is sailing at about 100° to 140° from the wind. The sails are approximately three-quarters of the way out.

6. Run: The stern faces the wind. While technically a Run extends to 180° from the wind, it is more comfortable and stable if the boat is sailing about 150° to 170° from the wind direction. The sails are between three-quarters and all the way out, perpendicular to the centerline of the boat.

Most sailboats cannot sail closer than 45° to the wind direction. For this reason, this area is called the No-Go Zone.

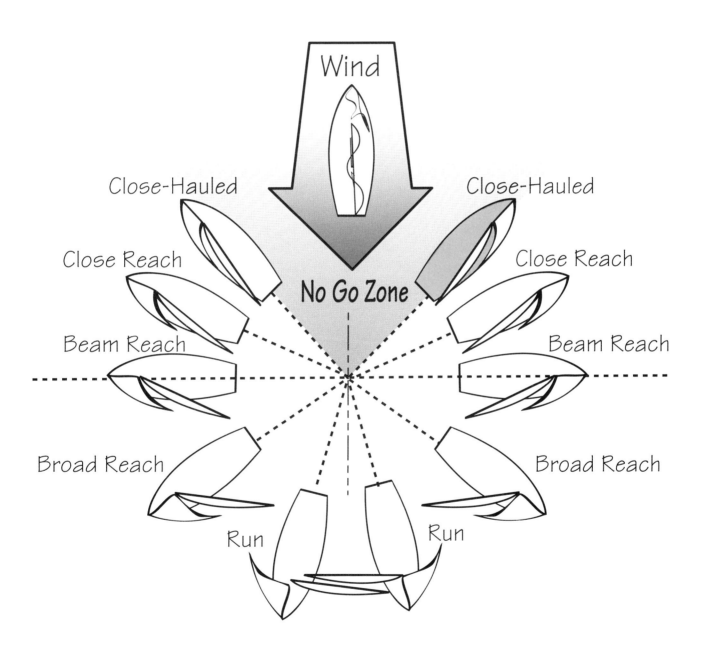

Wind

Close-Hauled   Close-Hauled

Close Reach   Close Reach

No Go Zone

Beam Reach   Beam Reach

Broad Reach   Broad Reach

Run   Run

Steering and sail trim (see chapter 8) are closely linked. Effective steering requires coordination between helmsman and crew:

• The helmsman steers and often assumes the skipper's role of being in charge. The helmsman usually trims the mainsheet.

• The crew trims the jib, balances the boat and keeps a keen lookout for things the helmsman may not see, creating a picture of what is happening outside of the boat.

Proper Position in the Boat

When you are steering the boat, sit facing the mainsail on the windward side just forward of the tiller so you can freely move the tiller as far as it will go from side to side. In this position, you will have a clear view of the trim of your sails and of the waters ahead. You will also be able to adjust your weight for boat balance from side to side, as well as fore and aft.

Grasp the mainsheet in your forward hand so the sheet leads up through your closed fist with the loose end over the top of your thumb. This grip allows you to comfortably hold the sheet and trim the mainsheet with your tiller hand as you steer.

When you are crewing, sit just forward of the skipper with your weight close together. The crew has a role equally important to that of the helmsman. You must constantly monitor the angle of heel and keep the boat from tipping too much. Move your weight in and out to keep the boat fairly flat on a steady angle of heel.

Tiller and Rudder Steering

Some beginners are surprised to find that the boat turns opposite to the direction they move the tiller. For example, if you move the tiller to starboard the boat will turn to port.

You steer with the tiller, but the rudder actually does the work of turning the boat. The rudder can only turn the boat if it is moving. If the boat is stopped, it will not turn.

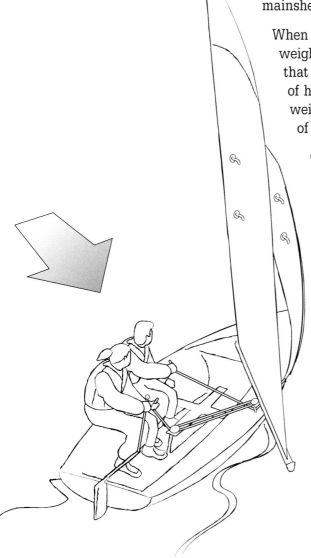

Heading Up and Heading Down

If you **push the tiller** toward the boom, the boat heads up toward the direction the wind is coming from.

If you **pull the tiller** away from the boom, the boat heads down (also known as bearing off) away from the wind direction.

A tiller extension enables you to steer while sitting farther forward and away from the tiller itself. This is very useful when hiking (sitting out on the side of the boat), which is necessary to flatten the heel of the boat in stronger wind. Hold the extension tiller like a microphone with your thumb near the end.

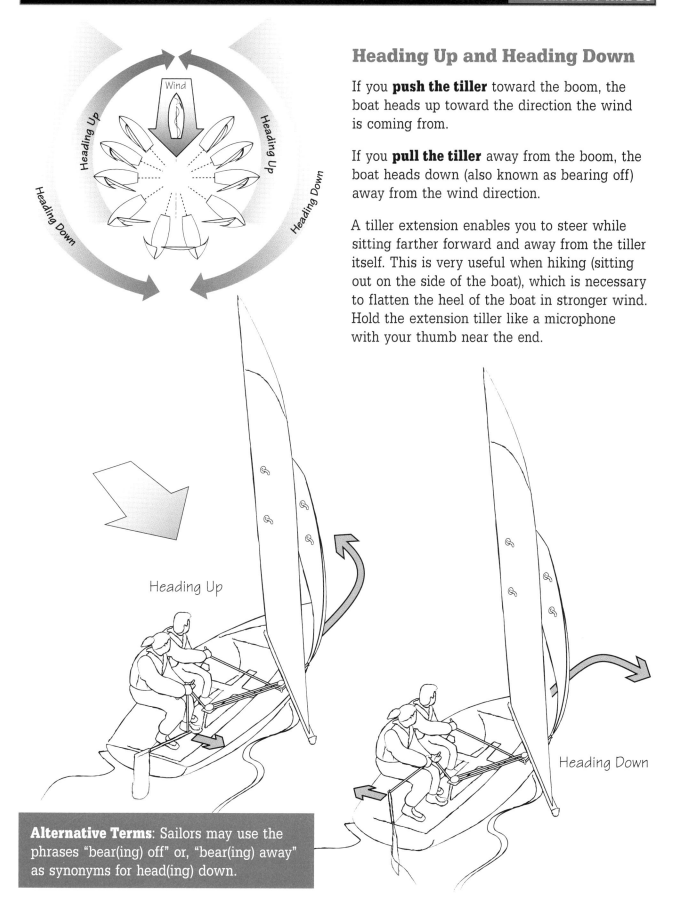

Alternative Terms: Sailors may use the phrases "bear(ing) off" or, "bear(ing) away" as synonyms for head(ing) down.

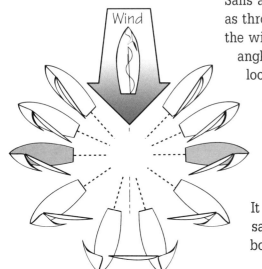

Sails are the engine of the boat. The wind is the fuel. You use the sheets as throttles to speed up or slow the boat by adjusting the angle at which the wind hits the sails. In the last chapter you learned to adjust the wind angle by steering toward or away from the wind. In this chapter we will look at adjusting the sails to the course you are sailing.

The **helmsman trims (adjusts) the mainsail using the mainsheet** and when sailing a crewed boat communicates changes of course or sail trim. The **crew trims the jib using the jibsheets.** The sheets are held at all times, even if cleated, in order to quickly respond to puffs and lulls and make necessary adjustments.

It is easiest to get the feel of steering and trimming sails together by sailing on a **beam reach** with the wind coming over the side of the boat at about 90°. You will set the **sails about halfway out.**

Alternative Terms:
Sail trimming terms vary among sailors:

To pull in a sailor may say **"Trim in"** or **"Sheet in."**

To let out the sail, a sailor may say **"Ease out"** or **"Sheet out."**

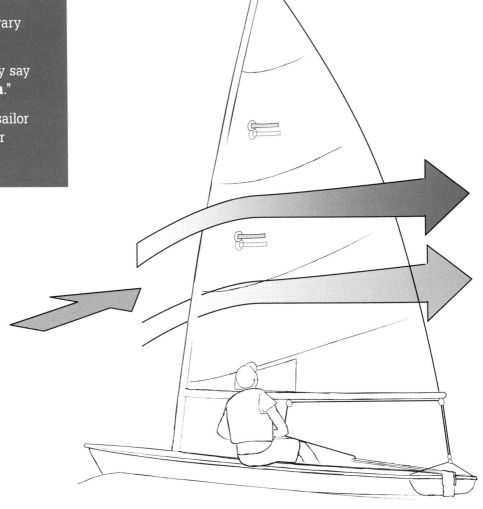

To Trim:

1. Just Right: You can find the basic, proper sail trim for upwind sailing and beam reaching by letting the sails out until they just start to luff – the leading edge flutters or looks like it's beginning to "boil" {see middle illustration} – and then trimming in slowly until the luffing stops. Proper sail trim will make the boat go faster. For downwind sailing, set the sails at right angles to the wind.

One aid to sail trim is the trimtale. Trimtales are pieces of yarn or cloth attached to both sides of the sail near the luff. Trim the sail so that the trimtales on both sides of the sail stream straight back. This is the optimum setting for the sail.

2. Too little trim: Luffing is a sign of uneven air flow over the sail with too little pressure on the windward side. The windward trimtale will flutter around. Trim the sail slightly until the trimtales stream to correct the problem. Undertrimming slows the boat and positions the sail too far out. You can do this on purpose to slow down, or reduce heel.

3. Too much trim: If the sheet is too tight, you are overtrimming the sail. The sail won't luff, but the air flow puts too much pressure on the windward side of the sail. The leeward trimtale will flutter or droop. Ease the sail to correct the problem. Overtrimming not only slows the boat but can cause it to heel more.

Use trimtales for better sail trim. The yarns or ribbons show the airflow over both sides of the sail.

Heeling and Hiking

Heeling to leeward – the tipping of the boat away from the wind – is normal. Heeling is caused by the pressure of the wind pushing on the sails, especially when sailing upwind. As wind pressure increases, the windward side of the hull rises.

In stronger winds, sailors need to **hike out** (lean out) while sitting on the windward side of the hull to counteract the heeling force of the wind in the sails, flattening the boat to keep it level.

A flatter boat is easier to steer.

Upwind Sailing

Start on a beam reach (90° to the wind) with proper sail trim and head up, turning the boat a little bit toward the wind (about 60° to 80° to the wind). The sails will begin to luff. You need to trim in the sails for the new point of sail, a close reach.

If you continue to head up to about 45° and trim in the sails to their tightest position, the boat is sailing close-hauled. This is as close to the wind as a boat can sail effectively.

When you are close-hauled, steer to keep the mainsail on the verge of a luff with trimtales streaming straight, since the sail is already pulled in as tight as practical (see page 22 and 40).

1. When close-hauled, if the sail luffs turn away from the wind slightly (move the tiller away from the boom toward the fluttering trimtale).

2. When close-hauled, if the leeward trimtale flutters or droops, turn toward the wind slightly (move the tiller toward the drooping trimtale).

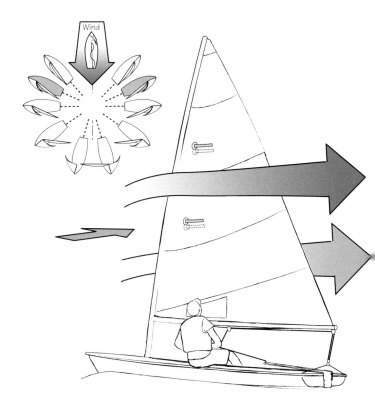

Downwind Sailing

Start on a beam reach with the sails trimmed properly. Head down, slowly pulling the tiller away from the boom, so the wind blows over the windward stern corner of the boat (about 100° to 150° off the wind). This is a broad reach. Keep your trimtales streaming back by letting the sails out until they are almost luffing.

As a broad reach becomes a run, the wind starts to push on the mainsail rather than flow along it, as pictured.

If you sail with the wind coming over the stern (170° off the wind to stay most comfortable), the boat is running (on a run). On this point of sail, the wind pushes only on the windward side of the sail and does not flow over both sides. The trimtales on the sails do not stream aft anymore. Set the boom at about right angles (90°) to the wind and pay careful attention to the trimtales on your shrouds to keep the wind coming over your windward stern corner. This will prevent an accidental jibe (see page 47).

Before getting underway, your boat may be in any number of places: at a dock, on the beach, on a trailer or on a mooring. You may have to launch the boat via a ramp or crane, or take a tender to get to it.

In any case, you can apply what you have learned to get underway.

Be prepared for sun, cold, wet and thirst (see chapter 1).

Be familiar with the boat and the equipment (see chapter 2).

Be aware of the area where you are sailing (see chapter 3).

Rig the boat thoroughly (see chapter 4).

Know the wind direction, tide, current and weather (see chapter 5).

Remember the points of sail and No-Go zone (see chapter 6).

Make sure the helmsman and crew know their jobs for steering, sail trim, looking out and communicating (see chapters 7 and 8).

Remember to:

- Make sure you are wearing your PFD.

- Step into the middle of the boat to keep your balance. Hold on to the deck or mast for support.

- Check that the "board" is down and the rudder and tiller are in place ready to use.

- Stow your personal gear – usually toward the bow.

- Raise the sails, if you haven't already.

- Coil (see page 51) the halyards.

- Check that everyone is ready.

- Untie the boat and push off.

WIND

Plan your departure:

Before setting sail, determine where you want to go and how you plan to get there. Whether leaving a dock, a beach or a mooring you will need some room to get into the boat, trim your sails and gain some speed so you can steer the boat. Choose a route that allows you the most time and opportunity before you encounter an obstacle, whether that is another boat, shallow water or anything else that will force you to turn in avoidance. Make sure your crew knows the plan before you depart!

Now it is Time to Go Sailing!

As you prepare to go aboard the boat, find the No-Go Zone and point the bow into the wind or place the boat in the safety position (see page 22), all sheets and the boom vang should be loose so the sails will luff. Take your time going aboard the boat, with the skipper getting into position first. When the boat is ready to go, push off to get moving, get into your proper positions and trim in the sails.

The helmsman should sit on the windward side, holding the mainsheet and the tiller as the sail fills. Steer the boat to sail your planned route. Locate a point in the distance to aim for, one that gives a clear path to steer and is more than 45° from the wind direction. Make sure the crew knows your plan and any changes you end up making along the way.

The crew should be the one to push the boat off before getting into position on board. The bow needs to be pushed all the way out of the No-Go Zone – at least 45° from the wind. To balance the boat, the crew can move to windward or leeward to keep the boat at a level heel while trimming the jibsheet.

The boat will pick up speed.

YOU'RE SAILING!

Leaving a dock from the windward side can be tricky, and requires careful timing. At the same time, you will need to be ready to sail upwind immediately as you leave. If you aren't prepared, the wind will tend to push you back onto the dock. If possible, move your boat to the leeward side and leave from there.

Step 1 As you raise your sails, make sure they are sheeted all-the-way out so they don't fill with wind.

Step 2 Push forward and away from the dock with enough speed to achieve steering and keep the boat from slideslipping back into the dock.

Step 3 Quickly trim in your sails for upwind sailing

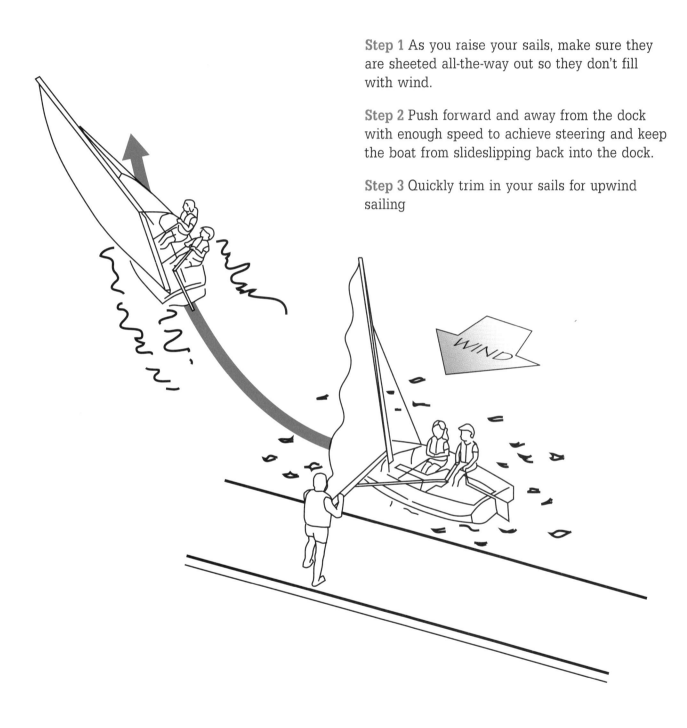

Pay attention to the basics:

- Look where you are going.

- Watch for other boats to prevent collision.

- Know the wind direction.

- Balance the boat to reduce heel.

- Match your sail trim to your point of sail.

- Try not to oversteer or make sudden movements with the tiller.

As you have figured out by now, sailing skills can be learned one at a time, but the time comes when they must be used in combination. This is a creative and fun part of sailing. Like any new physical or mental activity, the first time you try to put it all together can feel awkward or challenging. Don't worry, you have the ability to control the boat and the sails. You can stop and start as you wish. You can steer and trim sails. On your first sail, practice what you have learned so far.

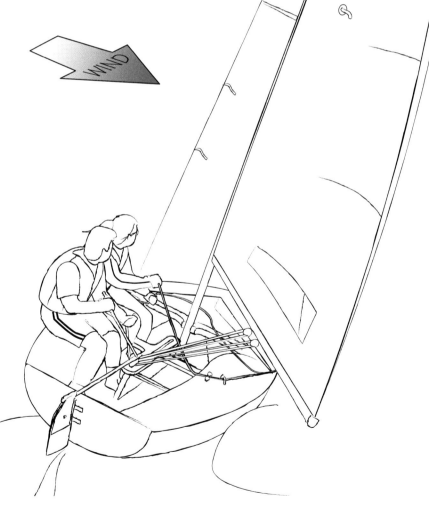

Steering

Once under sail, the helmsman can practice steering. At first, try to sail on a **beam reach**. Steer as straight as possible. Then try turning up to a close reach, back to a beam reach, and down a little bit onto a broad reach. Adjust the sails as you change course. Only small tiller adjustments (a few inches either way) are needed to make these changes in point of sail. Large movements of the tiller are needed when changing direction to tack or to avoid a collision.

Notice:

- How much movement of the tiller it takes to make the bow turn fast or slow.

- How much time elapses from the moment you turn the tiller until the bow starts to turn.

- How the boat continues to turn a little more after you center the tiller.

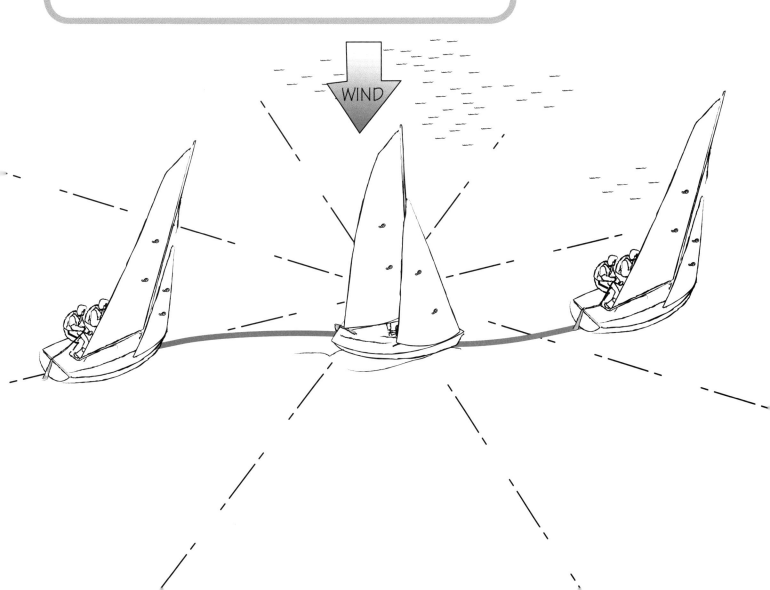

Trimming Tips

Most times when you head up, the sails will need to be trimmed in to stop luffing.

Most times that you bear off, let out the sails to prevent them from becoming over-trimmed.

Sails work at their maximum efficiency when they are on the verge of a luff.

When broad reaching or running, the sails may lose their ability to luff. Ease the sails out all the way to the shrouds (or perpendicular to the boat) to prevent over-trimming.

Sail Trim

On a **beam reach**, trim the sails about halfway out – mainsail and jib almost the same – just on the verge of luffing. Keep the trimtales streaming straight back. While steering a beam reach course, practice easing out the sheets and trimming them in while watching the trimtales for signs of luffing.

When the boat heads up to a **close reach**, you will notice that your sails start to luff and the windward/inside telltales flutter. This indicates that you need to trim in the sails. The boat may heel more and the wind may feel stronger. When the boat heads down to a **broad reach** you will notice that nothing changes in the appearance in the sails. They will not start to luff. However, the leeward/outside trimtales may start to flutter, indicating that the sails are trimmed too tightly and not performing efficiently. Proper adjustment for overtrimmed sails means that you need to let out the sails to adjust to the new wind angle. Let the sails out just far enough to luff, then trim back in until the luffing stops and both trimtales are streaming. The boat will heel less, and the wind will feel lighter.

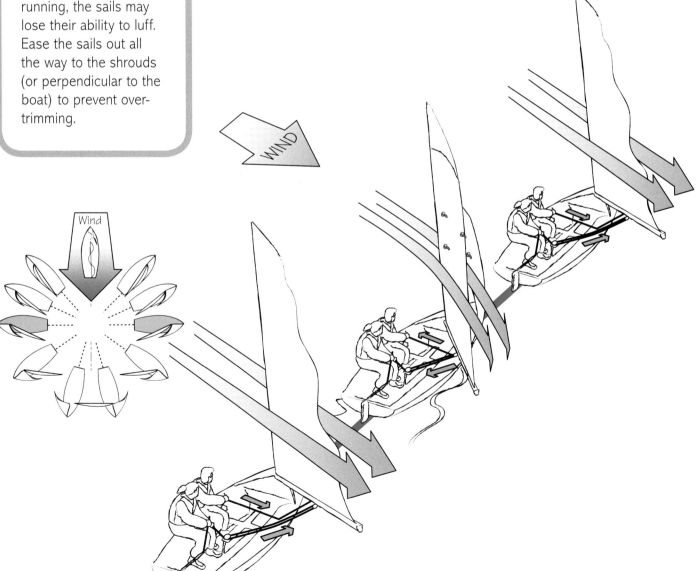

Getting In and Out of Irons

"Being **in irons**" describes a boat that is stopped, pointing into the No-Go Zone, with the sails luffing. You will not be able to steer normally.

If the boat does not have a jib, back the mainsail by pushing the boom forward on the side you want to turn to and hold the tiller in that same direction. As the boat begins to sail backwards, the bow will turn toward the boom, and away from the wind.

On a boat with a jib you can turn the bow away from the wind by backing the jib. To back the jib, hold it out to the side of the boat opposite the direction you want to go. The wind will push against the jib and turn the bow around without the boat backing up very much.

With either method, when the wind starts coming over the windward side of the boat, release the backed sail and pull in the sheets to stop the luffing. Pull the tiller away from the boom and continue sailing.

Trimtale Installation

If your sails do not have trimtales, you can put them on.

On the Jib: 7-9 inches back from the luff, ¼ and ½ of the way up the sail from the tack.

On the Mainsail: 12-14 inches back from the luff, ¼ and ½ of the way up the sail from the tack.

Trimtale Guide

Trimtales **streaming straight back:** good trim.

Windward trimtale dances or droops: trim in the sail or head down by moving the tiller slightly toward the fluttering trimtale.

Leeward trimtale dances or droops: ease out the sails or move the tiller slightly toward the fluttering/drooping trimtale.

When backing the sails, be aware that there will be wind pressure pushing back against you. The stronger the wind, the greater the pressure. Take care!

Avoiding Irons

The boat needs to be moving well and turned fairly quickly to glide through the No-Go zone. Otherwise, the boat will stop in the No-Go Zone, and you will have to get out of irons.

After learning to steer and trim the sails on a reach, the time will come to turn around and sail back to where you started. To turn around you will **tack**.

When **tacking**, the bow heads up and coasts **through the entire 90° No-Go Zone**. This maneuver is also called **coming about**.

In order to tack, the **helmsman** prepares the crew, then pushes the tiller hard to leeward. The bow turns through the wind until the sails fill on the other side. Center the tiller as soon as the mainsail has filled with wind. The boat will start to sail in the new direction.

The **crew** follows the helmsman's directions to tack, trimming the active sheet on the leeward side as the boat heads into the wind. Once the jib luffs in the middle of the boat, the crew releases the old sheet and trims the new one to the appropriate point of sail.

Alternative Terms: Traditionally, sailors say **"Ready about?"** before tacking and **"Hard-to-lee"** as they turn the boat.

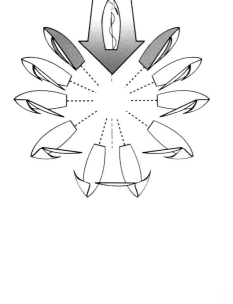

Wind

WIND

NO-GO ZONE

Finish

Helmsman: As the mainsail fills, center the tiller and steer to the new course. As you sit down, take the mainsheet from your tiller hand with your forward hand.

Crew: Adjust the active jibsheet to properly trim the jib for the new point of sail. Move to a position where you can keep the boat from heeling too much and sit down.

Step 3: Changing Sides

Helmsman: As the boat passes through head-to-wind, the boom crosses the boat. Face forward and keep your head down as you step across the boat (leading with your aft foot). Steer with the tiller behind your back. Bring the hand holding the mainsheet back to the tiller/tiller extension (both are now in your aft hand).

Crew: Facing forward, move across the boat to help balance its heel while trimming in the new, active jibsheet.

Step 2: Turning

Helmsman: Say "Tacking" or "Hard-to-Lee." Push the tiller firmly to leeward.

Crew: When you hear "Tacking," watch for the jib to luff as the boat comes head-to-wind. Then release the "active" jibsheet as it goes slack.

Step 1: Preparation

Helmsman: Look to windward and astern to check for traffic or obstacles. Hold the mainsheet in your forward hand. When the way is clear, ask your crew: "Ready to tack?"

Crew: When you hear "Ready to tack?" grasp the new "inactive" jibsheet and continue holding the "active" leeward jibsheet. When you are prepared, respond by saying "Ready!"

For better execution on the water, practice maneuvers on land.

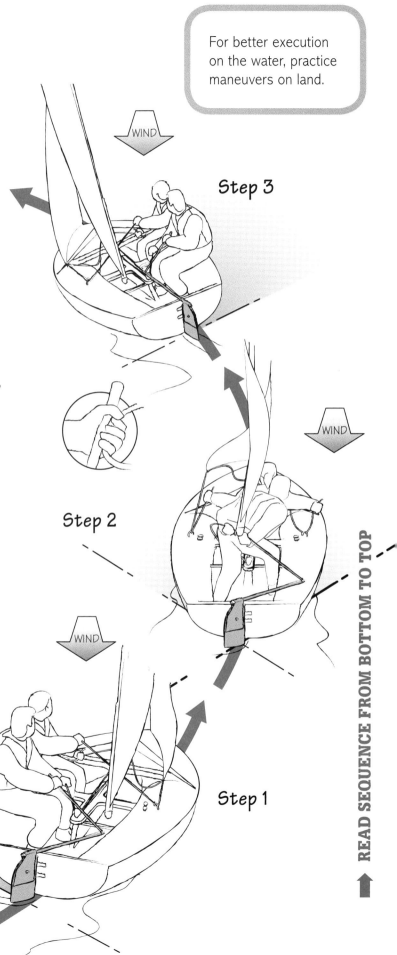

Step 3

Step 2

Step 1

READ SEQUENCE FROM BOTTOM TO TOP

Upwind sailing requires careful coordination between sail trim and steering. You cannot always point the boat where you want to go. Tacking takes you from one edge of the No-Go Zone to the other as you zigzag your way to windward.

To sail upwind, steer as close to the edge of the No-Go Zone as possible. Trim the mainsail and jib in close, but not until they are board-flat. The challenge falls to the helmsman to keep the sails on the edge of luffing by watching the trimtales and steering to keep the sails full even when the wind shifts slightly back and forth. This is called sailing **in the groove**.

Finding the Groove

The groove is the narrow, close-hauled course just on the edge of the No-Go Zone.

High of the groove – too close to the wind – the sails luff and the boat slows.

Low of the groove – toward a close reach – you are sailing extra distance to get to your upwind destination.

Beating Upwind Through a Series of Tacks

A boat can't sail straight upwind because of the No-Go Zone. To get to an upwind destination, sail close-hauled on one tack and then the other – back and forth in a zigzag – to work your way to windward. It is like turning left and right repeatedly on a grid of streets to move diagonally across town or like using switchbacks to bike or hike up a mountain. This is known as beating upwind.

Whether you are trying to go upwind or just sailing back and forth, tacking is a great skill to practice while getting a feel for steering and balancing a boat in different wind speeds and water conditions.

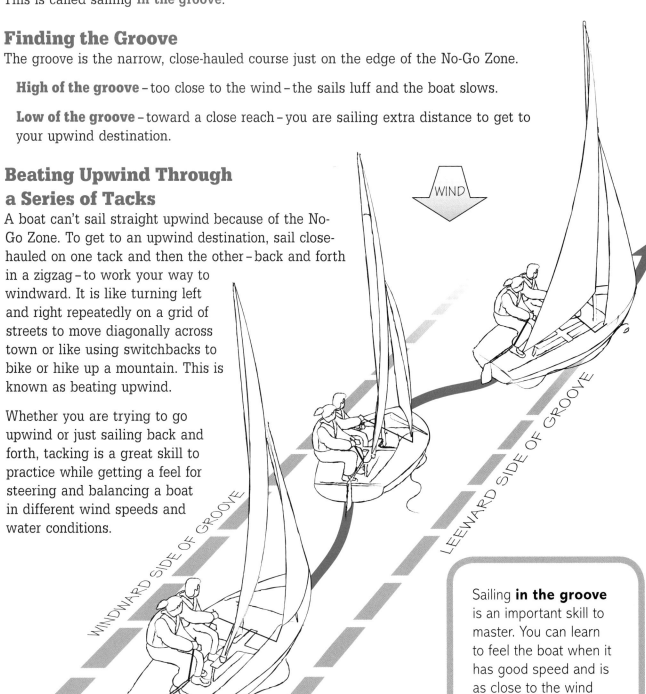

WIND

WINDWARD SIDE OF GROOVE

LEEWARD SIDE OF GROOVE

Sailing **in the groove** is an important skill to master. You can learn to feel the boat when it has good speed and is as close to the wind as possible.

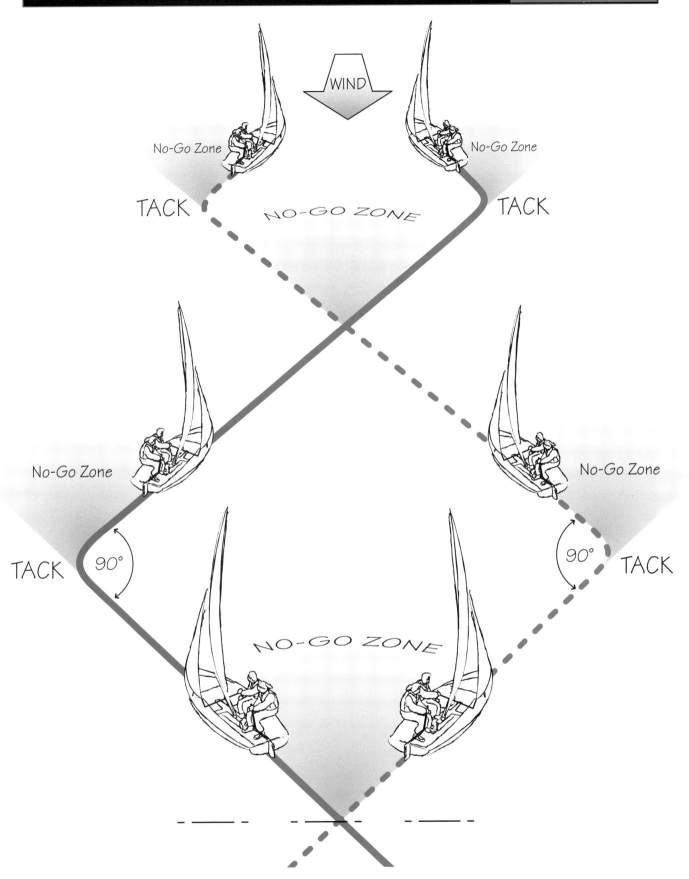

Putting On the Brakes

To **stop the boat** when sailing downwind you should steer back toward a close reach to luff the sails. The sails can't luff when sailing downwind.

To **slow the boat** when sailing downwind, over-trim the sails by pulling them in to a close-hauled setting.

Even if you have never sailed before, you already know the sensation of sailing downwind from walking on a windy day with the wind at your back. If you spread your coat out, you are pushed from behind. The same concept is at work in downwind sailing.

As you head downwind from a beam reach to a run, the wind's effect on the sail changes from flowing around both sides to pushing against the windward side. The trimtales on the sail are no longer useful. They will hang limply.

You must keep track of the wind angle by keeping a watchful eye on wind indicators other than the sail. Feel the wind on the back of your neck, look at a trimtale tied to the shroud or watch little ripples on the water. With the wind pushing on the mainsail, you should let out the mainsheet until the boom is at approximately a right angle to the wind. Let the jib out about the same amount.

Broad Reaching

When broad reaching, the wind comes over the aft windward corner of the hull. Balancing the boat is important because as a boat turns away from the wind it has a tendency to roll to windward or leeward and become less stable. On a windy day, reaching is safer than running because the boat is more stable and rocks less. It is also easier to avoid an uncontrolled or accidental jibe (see page 47) on this point of sail.

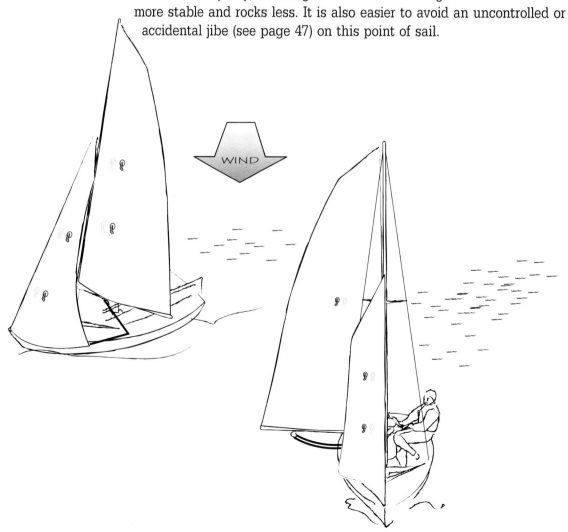

Running

When running, the **wind comes over the stern** along the centerline of the boat. Both the helmsman and crew are usually sitting in the cockpit or on opposite sides of the boat for balance because hiking isn't needed. The boom is pushed out as far as it will go – to the shroud or about 90° from the centerline. The jib may just hang limply because the mainsail blocks all the wind, or it may be set on the windward side to help catch more wind.

The **helmsman** may find that steering on a run becomes more difficult, especially if the boat rolls with the waves. This point of sail requires paying close attention to wind direction. Accurate steering keeps the wind from coming from the opposite/leeward side of the mainsail, forcing the boom to swing across the cockpit in an **accidental jibe** (see page 47). If the jib goes limp, you are sailing in jibing territory, so head up a little (push the tiller toward the boom). Downwind sailing is safer on a broad reach.

Controlled Jibing

In jibing, the boat heads away from the wind with the wind crossing from one corner of the stern to the other. At the same time, the boom changes sides of the boat. The helmsman pulls in the mainsheet before the jibe and lets it out very quickly as the boom changes sides. The tiller only needs to be turned a little to make the jibe smooth and controlled.

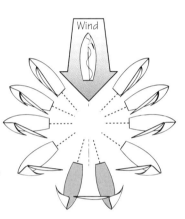

Accidental Jibe

If you sail on a run, the wind can catch the back/leeward side of the main-sail and push the boom across to the other side of the boat unexpectedly. This could cause you to lose control of the boat.

Step 1: Preparation
Helmsman

- Look around to check for traffic or obstacles.
- Check the wind direction.
- Choose a direction to steer after the jibe.
- Ask your crew "Ready to jibe?"

Crew

- Hold both jibsheets.
- Crew responds with "Ready" when prepared.

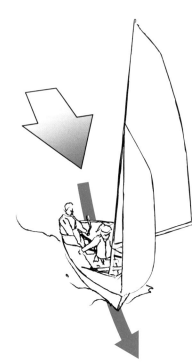

Step 1: Preparation

Step 2: Turn the Boat
Helmsman

- Say "Jibing" while turning slowly downwind.
- Trim in the mainsail partway so the boom is over the cockpit.

Crew

- Stay low for better balance and to avoid the boom.
- Trim the jib by using the "new" sheet.

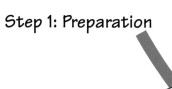

Step 2: Turn the boat

The Helmsman Duties: Think it through before you start. First, sail onto a deep broad reach or near run by slowly pulling the tiller away from the mainsail to turn downwind. Continue to watch for obstructions. Trim the mainsheet as you continue turning the boat to a run. As the boom crosses the centerline, immediately center the tiller, duck under the boom and cross the cockpit. You will learn to change hands for the sheet and tiller behind your back without looking down.

The Crew Duties: Tend the jib and shift weight to flatten heeling.

> **Alternative Terms:** Traditionally, sailors say **"Ready to jibe?"** and then **"Jibe-ho"** – meaning "jibing" – as they turn the boat. Whichever term you choose, make sure your crew hears it in time to prepare and safely duck under the boom through the maneuver.

Step 3: Boom Swings Across

Helmsman

- Stay low for better balance and to avoid the boom.
- Change sides leading with aft foot.
- Center the tiller as boom crosses the centerline.
- Ease mainsail quickly.

Crew

- Duck under the boom.
- Balance the boat through the jibe.

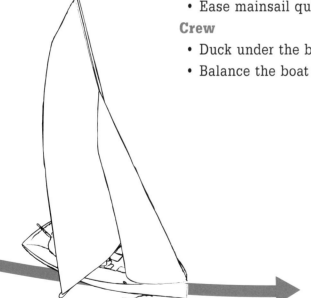

Steer New Course

Helmsman

- Check the wind direction for proper sail trim.

Crew

- Check the sail for proper jib trim.

Step 3: Boom swings across

Helm-Hand Exchange While Jibing *(Read sequence from bottom to top)*

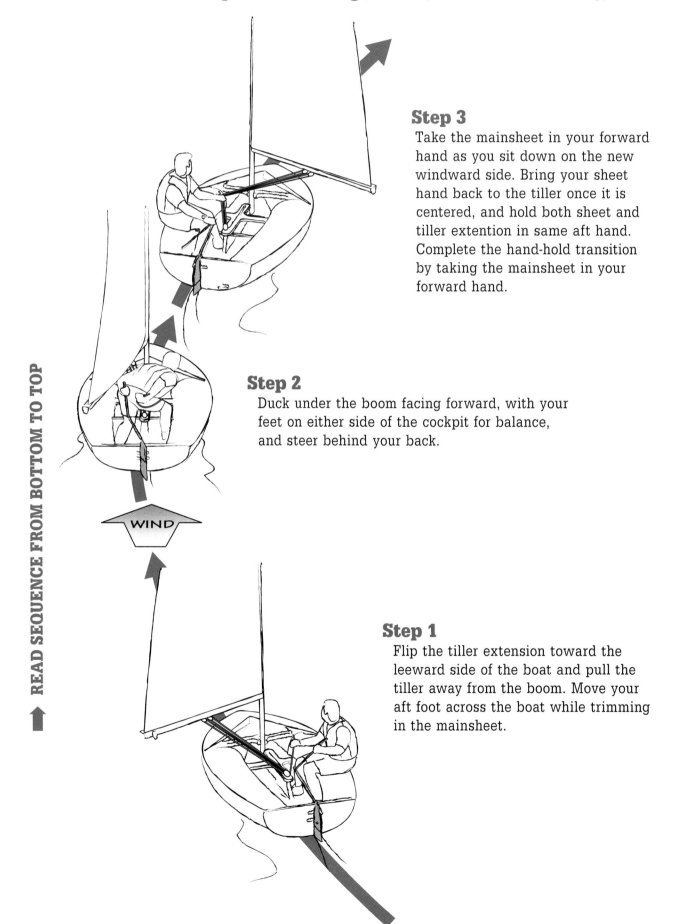

READ SEQUENCE FROM BOTTOM TO TOP

WIND

Step 3

Take the mainsheet in your forward hand as you sit down on the new windward side. Bring your sheet hand back to the tiller once it is centered, and hold both sheet and tiller extention in same aft hand. Complete the hand-hold transition by taking the mainsheet in your forward hand.

Step 2

Duck under the boom facing forward, with your feet on either side of the cockpit for balance, and steer behind your back.

Step 1

Flip the tiller extension toward the leeward side of the boat and pull the tiller away from the boom. Move your aft foot across the boat while trimming in the mainsheet.

Accidental Jibe

If you accidentally sail past 180° or let the stern turn so the wind is on the same side of the boat as the boom, the boom could accidentally swing across the boat uncontrolled – very fast and hard. The boat can roll wildly. Someone might get hurt or some part of the rigging might be damaged. A capsize is possible. All are good reasons to avoid an uncontrolled jibe.

If you do jibe accidentally, steer straight on a broad reach to regain control and settle the boat down. You can then plan a controlled jibe to get back on course.

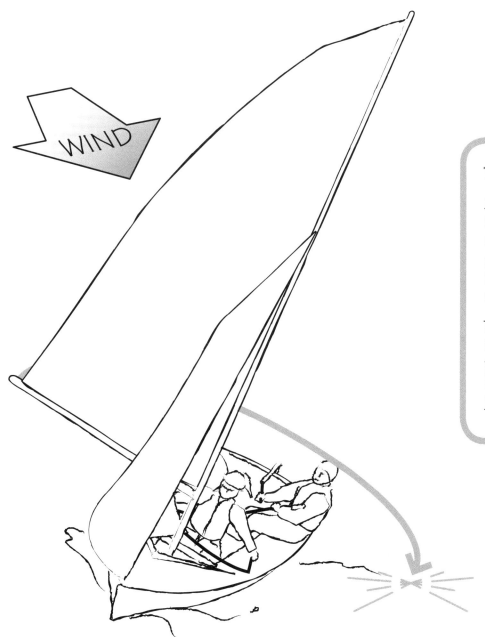

Tiller Control

Jibing needs much less tiller movement than tacking – only a few degrees rather than pushing the tiller all the way to one side.

To control the jibe, trim in the mainsail before you jibe, but quickly release the sheet after the jibe is complete.

Every sailing experience ends with a return to shore. You will use your skills in steering and controlling boat speed to approach the dock, float, mooring or beach from which you departed. As you sail toward your landing point, plan your preferred approach and landing, as well as an escape plan in case things do not go as anticipated.

Landings

Be sure you know where the water is too shallow for sailing, especially in a tidal area with changeable depth. You may need to raise the centerboard and the rudder to avoid hitting bottom as you approach the shore.

Double-check the wind direction to plan your approach. If it is possible, approach the leeward side of a dock with the windward side of the boat. This way you can use the safety position to control your speed and heading as you glide to a stop at your "parking space." This approach can also work for a beach. Once near the beach, the crew can jump out to hold the bow into the wind.

The wind doesn't always cooperate. In calm conditions, you may need to paddle the boat to your destination. Sometimes you will have to land with the wind blowing onto the beach or dock. With improved boat handling, you will learn how to do this yourself.

Preparing to Land

- Plan your approach.

- Have an escape route if the landing is not going well.

- Sail in slowly when you are ready.

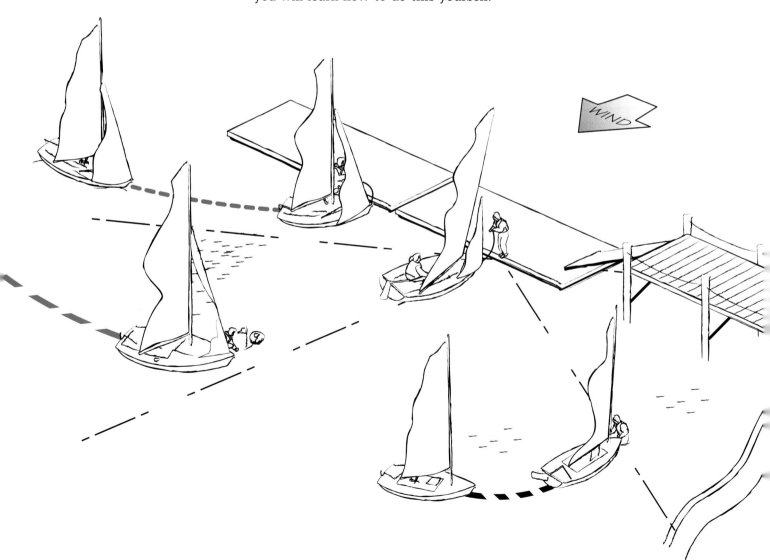

Windward Return - Approaching a Dock

Similar to leaving a dock from the windward side, returning to the windward side can be challenging. Whenever possible, try to return on the leeward side of the dock. If returning to the windward side is necessary, use the Windward Side Approach.

Note: When coming back to a dock, it is not unusual to find the wind blowing from a different direction than when you left, so you may have to make your landing on a different side. For this reason, you should always think ahead and have a firm plan of how to leave and return to the dock safely from all directions.

Windward Side Approach

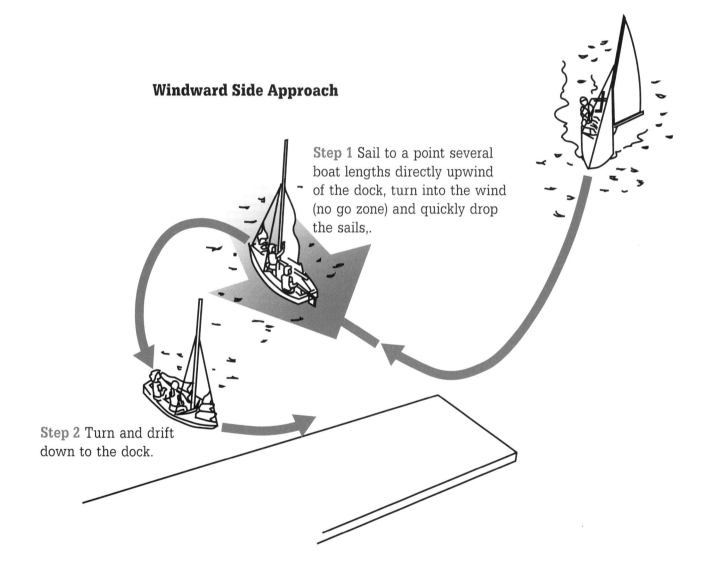

Step 1 Sail to a point several boat lengths directly upwind of the dock, turn into the wind (no go zone) and quickly drop the sails,.

Step 2 Turn and drift down to the dock.

Shipshape

Leave the boat clean, tidy and safely secured

- Bail and dry cockpit
- Tie off halyards
- Stow rudder and tiller
- Remove or raise board
- Put away sails
- Remove personal gear
- Return PFDs
- Remove tank plugs and drain hull if the boat is stored ashore

Lowering Sail

In most cases, the boat should be tied to the dock or mooring before lowering the sails. On a beach, you may slide the boat ashore before taking the sails down.

Make sure the halyards are untangled and free to run. Lower the sails in the reverse order that they were raised: mainsail down first, then jib. Support the boom to keep it from dropping as the main halyard is lowered. Secure both ends of the halyards when you take them off the sails.

If the sails are dry, put them away as you found them. Either roll them by starting at the head and keeping the battens parallel to the foot, or fold ("flake") the sails instead. To fold the sail, start at the foot and make accordion pleats. Then start from the clew end and fold into a small square. Wet sails should be rinsed, if salty, and dried before putting them away.

If you have capsized and the mast or sail were muddied, be sure to wash them clean. Mud can dry nearly as hard as concrete and stain a sail. You may be asked to remove the rudder and tiller and raise the centerboard or daggerboard if the boat is not going to be used for a while. Coil up the halyards and sheets, and stow them so they can dry.

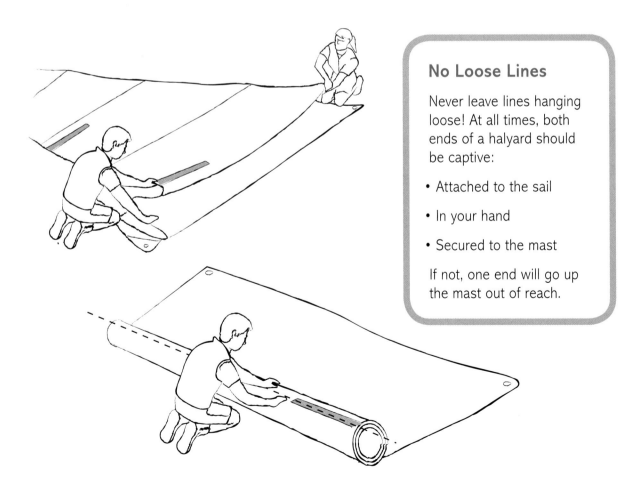

No Loose Lines

Never leave lines hanging loose! At all times, both ends of a halyard should be captive:

- Attached to the sail
- In your hand
- Secured to the mast

If not, one end will go up the mast out of reach.

Knots and Coiling

On boats, rope is called line (think "fishing line"). Tying knots and handling lines are a part of seamanship. Knots should be easy to tie and untie, and be suited to their purpose. Coiling will keep lines tidy until you need them.

Coiling keeps lines untangled and ready for use. A tangled halyard is a nuisance when you want to lower the sails quickly. Put a few wraps around the coil before hanging it up and out of the way.

A **Cleat Hitch** secures a line to a horn cleat, which is commonly found on docks to secure mooring lines and on boats to secure running rigging. First take a turn around the cleat and then figure-eight the line around the horns of the cleat. Finish with a twist (a half hitch), which captures the free end under itself so the hitch does not loosen.

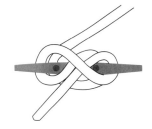

A **Figure-Eight** is a stopper knot used in the end of a line to keep the line – like a sheet or halyard – from pulling through a fitting or a block. The end of the line is passed over and then around itself and the end is pulled through the loop. Tie the knot about three or four inches from the end to keep it from working loose.

A **Square Knot** (a matched pair of overhand knots) is useful for tying two lines together quickly and easily.

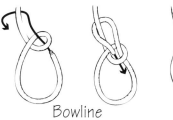

Bowline

A **Bowline** is the most useful knot in sailing. It is very secure and very easy to untie. Bowlines can be used to attach jibsheets to the jib clew or a docking line to a ring – anything that needs a secure loop.

A **Cow Hitch** is a very simple knot that can be used for jibsheets. Double a line, passing the loop through the grommet (eye) in the clew of the jib. Then pass both tail ends of the line through the loop to form the sheets.

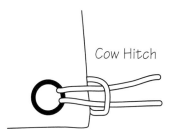

Cow Hitch

Courtesy on the water makes sailing more fun for everyone. Treat others as you would like to be treated. Beyond courtesy, there are the Navigation Rules – like traffic laws – that can be enforced by authorities.

The Navigation Rules help prevent accidents. The rules apply to the smallest rowboat and the largest tanker. In general, the Navigation Rules:

- Recognize that some vessels should be avoided by other vessels.
- Specify which of two vessels should "give way" to the other as they approach each other.
- Require every vessel to avoid collision even if they have the rights of the "stand-on" vessel.

Less experienced sailors should stay clear of boating traffic. Sail defensively.

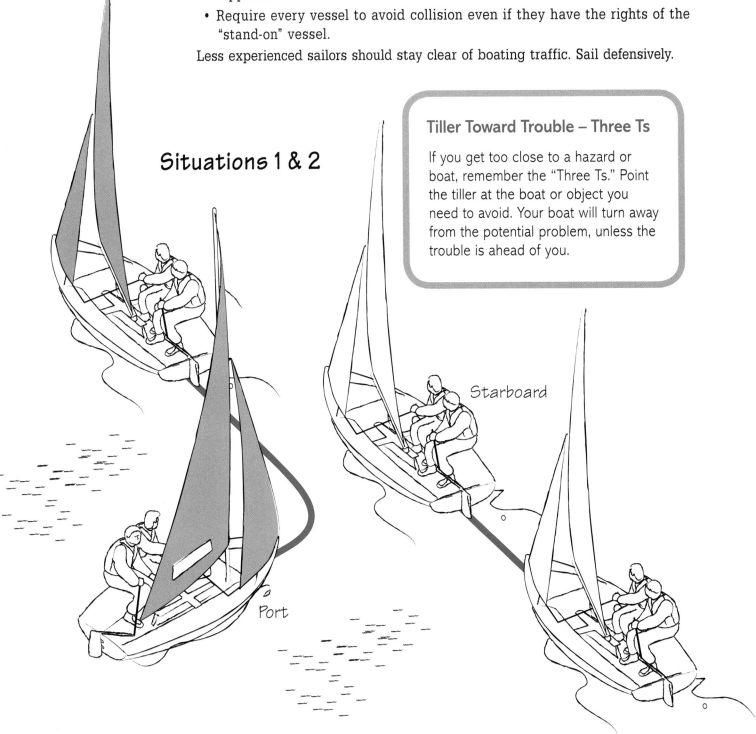

Situations 1 & 2

Tiller Toward Trouble – Three Ts

If you get too close to a hazard or boat, remember the "Three Ts." Point the tiller at the boat or object you need to avoid. Your boat will turn away from the potential problem, unless the trouble is ahead of you.

Starboard

Port

Five Basic Navigation Rules for Sailing Situations

1. If two vessels might come close or collide,
   - The "stand-on" vessel maintains course and speed.
   - The "give-way" vessel alters course and/or speed to pass at a safe distance.

2. Port-tack boat gives way to the starboard-tack boat – upwind or downwind.

3. Windward boat gives way to the leeward boat on the same tack, whether sailing upwind or downwind.

4. Overtaking boat gives way to the vessel ahead, whether a sailboat or powerboat.

5. Powerboat gives way to a sailboat. It's true most of the time. However, never push your luck. Stay away from power vessels and ships, especially in navigational channels.

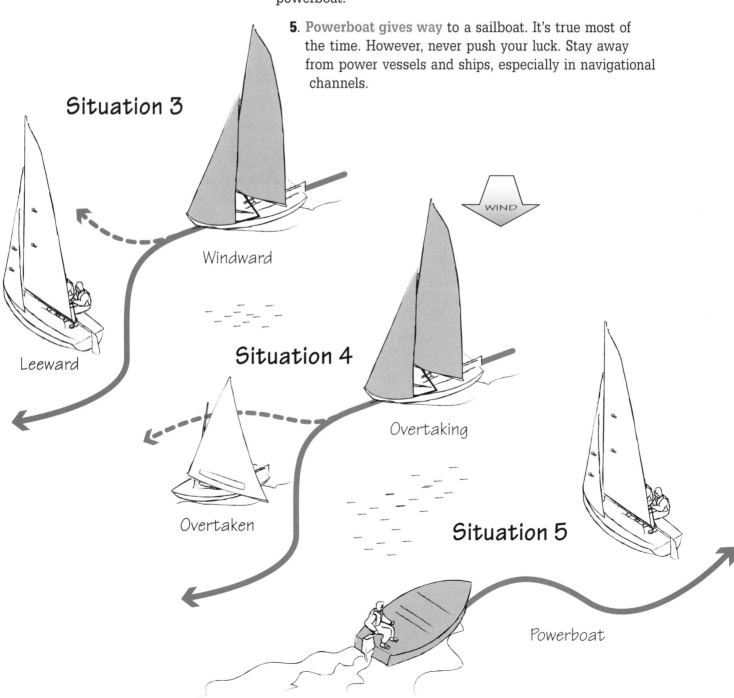

Situation 3

Windward

Leeward

WIND

Situation 4

Overtaking

Overtaken

Situation 5

Powerboat

Who has right-of-way?

Once you know the basics of sailing, you should learn a few seamanship skills. Good seamanship helps you handle situations even when you're not sailing. Your boat may need to be towed for some reason. You may need to paddle from a dock to a mooring. And, you may already have noticed the need for specific knots for specific jobs on board!

Water safety is always important. Sailors can unexpectedly find themselves in the water. The boat may capsize. The best sailors in the world have experienced capsizing and falling overboard. Wearing a PFD and being comfortable in the water make sailing a safer experience for every sailor.

Capsize Recovery – Scoop Method

Most often, when a boat tips over it capsizes to leeward because the force of the wind overcomes the ability of the crew to hike or let out the sails. It is important to practice capsize recovery drills before you need to use them on your own. Once the boat is on its side and the sails are in the water, you should act promptly to right the boat. The Scoop Method of recovery gets its name because one crew is "scooped" into the cockpit as the other rights the capsized boat.

Steps 1-2

Crew ("Scoopee")

1. Tread water near the stern until the scooper has control of the centerboard.
2. Move to centerboard trunk and free the mainsheet and jibsheets. If necessary, throw the windward jib sheet over the high side to the scooper to assist the Scooper in getting up on the board.

Skipper ("Scooper")

1. Move around the boat to the centerboard.
2. Climb up onto the board, using the jibsheet if necessary. Remember to avoid putting pressure on the tip of the board or you may break it.

Step 3

Crew ("Scoopee")

3. Hold on to a cockpit structure as the boat goes upright and get scooped in.

Skipper ("Scooper")

3. Once on the board make sure the scoopee is ready for the boat to be righted. Place your feet close to the base of the board where it enters the hull and lean back, bracing yourself with the tail end of a sheet or halyard for leverage, until the boat gradually comes upright.

Capsize Recovery Guidelines

- Stay with the boat.
- Check for injuries.
- Don't go under the boat or sails.

Step 4-5

Crew ("Scoopee")

4. Balance the boat and steer it into the safety position.

5. Help the scooper on board over the stern.

Skipper ("Scooper")

4. Swim to stern to climb back on board.

Person in the Water (PIW)

Someone may fall into the water while the boat is sailing. It is important to keep visual contact with the PIW and return to them as quickly and safely as possible. You need to tack the boat and sail back toward them on a close reach. Control your speed and glide to a stop. Stop the boat in the **safety position** (see page 22). Help the PIW on board just like the crew in the capsize drill. You already have learned all the skills necessary to retrieve someone in the water. In this drill, you just link the individual skills together.

Step 1: Figure-8 PIW Recovery: For the reach-tack-reach Figure-8 PIW Recovery, sail on a beam to broad reach away from the PIW and tack in approximately five to ten seconds. Maintain visual contact. Approach the PIW slowly on a close reach, gliding towards them in the safety position.

Step 2: Safety Position: Luff the sails and keep the PIW to windward.

Step 3: Retrieve the PIW: This procedure is the same for capsize or overboard retrievals. Assist the PIW into the boat over the stern.

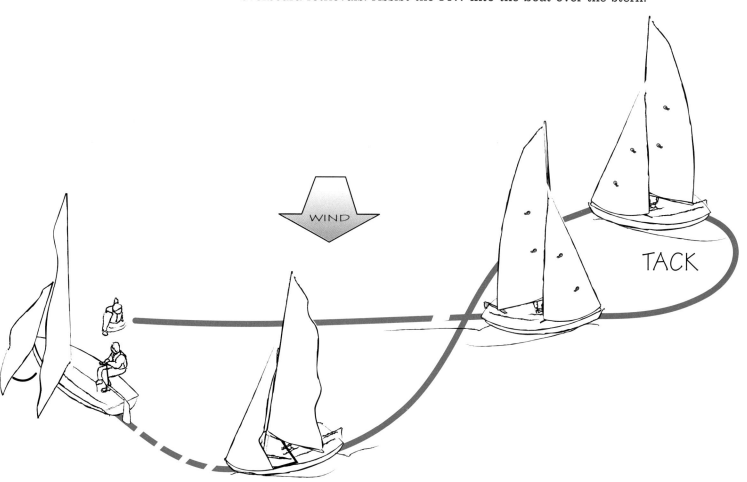

Towing

There are many reasons why a sailboat may need to be towed: the wind dies; the boat has a breakdown; bad weather or an emergency occurs. You need to know how to pick up a tow from another boat. The towline (rope) may be thrown to you or dragged in the water past your boat where you can reach it. Tie the towline around the mast at deck level using a bowline (see page 51).

Drop any sails that aren't supporting the rig and secure them in the cockpit. Raise the board halfway. Before the towboat takes up the strain on the towline, sit where you can balance the boat and steer directly behind the stern of the towing boat. If no tow boat is available, you can also use a paddle to propel a sailboat.

Abeam .... The location of anything beyond either side of the boat at right angles to the centerline.

Accidental jibe .... An unexpected jibe when sailing downwind and the wind catches the back side of the mainsail, possibly causing the helmsman to lose control of the boat.

Aft.. The direction toward the stern.

Ahead... The location of anything forward of the bow.

Astern .... The location of anything aft of the stern.

Battens .... Stiffening pieces placed horizontally along the leech of a sail.

Beam reach .... The point of sailing across the wind about 90° from the wind, with the sails approximately halfway out.

Boom.. A spar attached to the mast at right angles to hold the bottom of the mainsail.

Boom groove............................. A slot on the top side of the boom into which the foot of the mainsail slides.

Boom vang................................ A piece of running rigging that pulls down on the boom to keep it from rising under the pressure of the wind on the mainsail.

Bottom....................................... The outside surface of the hull below the water.

Bow.. The front of any hull.

Bowline..................................... The most useful knot in sailing, the bowline produces an eye that is very secure but very easy to untie.

Broad reach.............................. The downwind point of sailing about 100° to 140° from the wind, with the sails approximately three-quarters of the way out.

Catamaran................................ A type of multihull with two hulls.

Centerboard............................. A form of fin to prevent sideslip that is adjusted by swinging up and down in a trunk.

Centerline................................ The fore-and-aft line running from bow to stern halfway between the sides of the boat.

Cleat.. A fitting to which a piece of running rigging is secured.

Cleat hitch............................... The method of securing a line to a horn cleat by taking a turn around the cleat and then passing the line in a figure-eight pattern around the horns of the cleat.

Clew.. The corner of a sail between the leech and the foot.

Close-hauled .... The upwind point of sailing closest to the wind, about 45° from the wind direction, with the sails trimmed in close.

Close reach............................... The upwind point of sailing about 60° to 75° from the wind direction, with the sails let out a quarter of the way, just on the verge of luffing.

Cockpit...................................... The interior part of a boat where people usually sit.

Coming about.......................... *See* Tacking and "Hard-to-lee."

Controlled jibe........................ Allowing the boat to jibe while steering carefully and trimming the main sheet in and out smoothly.

Cow hitch .... A very simple loop knot often used to secure jib sheets to the clew of the jib.

Crew.. The person or persons in the boat who trim the jib, balance the boat and keep a lookout for things the helmsman may not see.

Cunningham .... A line or mechanism that tensions the forward edge of a sail.

Current...................................... The horizontal flow of water.

Daggerboard............................ A daggerboard slides up and down through the hull and acts like a centerboard to keep a sailboat from side-slipping.

Daggerboard trunk .... A slot through the hull that holds a daggerboard.

Downwind................................ The direction of movement with the wind coming over the stern.

Downwind sailing.................. Sailing in the direction to which the wind is blowing, which includes broad reaching and running.

Drain plugs.............................. Caps for the holes used to drain water from the cockpit, which must be inserted before sailing a boat stored on land.

Ease... To let out a sheet slowly and smoothly to find the optimum setting for a sail.

"Ease out".................................. A command for letting out a sheet to trim a sail.

Fairlead.. A small circular fitting through which a sheet may be led to keep it free for trimming.

Figure-eight knot .... A simple stopper knot tied in the end of a sheet to prevent it from slipping through a fairlead.

Figure-eight PIW .... (person in the water) recovery. A procedure for retrieving someone in the water by sailing a figure-eight pattern to return alongside and pick them up.

Fins .... Appendages to a hull for steering or to prevent sideslipping. *See Centerboard, Daggerboard, Keel, Leeboard, Rudder.*

Foot .... The bottom edge of a sail.

Forestay .... The piece of standing rigging that runs from the bow to the head of the mast to support it.

Forward .... The direction toward the bow.

Give-way vessel .... Under Navigation Rules, the vessel that must alter course and/or speed to pass at a safe distance.

Halyard .... A piece of running rigging used to raise a sail.

Hank .... A fitting on the luff of the jib that clips it to the forestay.

"Hard-to-lee"............................ The helmsman's warning when putting the helm down to tack through the wind.

Head... The top corner of a sail.

Head down .... To steer away from the wind direction by pulling the tiller away from the position of the boom.

Head off.................................... *See Head down.*

Head up..................................... To steer toward the wind direction by pushing the tiller toward the position of the boom.

Heel... The tipping of a boat away from the wind due to the pressure of the wind on the sails, especially when sailing upwind.

Helmsman .... The person who steers a boat and often assume's the skipper's position of being in charge. The helmsman usually trims the mainsheet.

High of the groove.................. A windward sailing course too close to the wind, in which the sails luff and the boat slows.

Hiking .... Sitting on the side of the boat to flatten the heel of the boat in stronger wind.

Hull .... The body of the boat, to which everything else is attached.

In irons..................................... The situation of a boat when the bow is turned into the No-Go Zone and the sails are luffing.

In the groove .... Sailing in the narrow, close-hauled course just on the edge of the No-Go Zone.

Jib... The triangular sail at a boat's bow, with its luff attached to the forestay.

Jib sheets................................. The two controlling lines for the jib, which are alternately eased and trimmed in as a boat changes tacks.

Jibe.. To change tacks when sailing downwind, with the wind over the stern, by allowing the wind to swing the boom from one side to the other.

"Jibe ho" .... The traditional command for beginning to jibe.

"Jibing"..................................... The helmsman's command when beginning to jibe.

Keel.. A type of underwater fin to prevent sideslip that is fixed to the hull and cannot be raised.

Leech .... The back edge of a sail.

Leeward (LOU-ward).............. The direction, in relation to the boat, opposite that from which the wind is blowing.

Leeward boat........................... Under Navigation Rules, the boat that maintains course and speed when meeting a windward boat on the same tack.

Line .... On boats, the term for rope.

Low of the groove................... A windward sailing course too far off the wind toward a close reach, requiring extra distance to reach a windward destination.

Luff.. The front edge of a sail.

Luffing.......................The fluttering of the forward edge (luff) of a sail when the boat is turned too far into the wind, resulting in too little pressure on the windward side of the sail.

Lull.............................A brief decrease in wind velocity.

Main............................*See Mainsail.*

Mainsail.......................In a single-masted boat, the principal sail, with its luff attached to the aft side of the mast and its foot attached to the boom.

Main sheet.....................The piece of running rigging that is attached to the boom to trim the mainsail.

Mast...........................The vertical spar that supports the sails and is supported by the standing rigging.

Mast groove....................A slot on the af side of the mast into which the luff of the mainsail slides.

Midships.......................The area of a boat about halfway between bow and stern.

Monohull.......................A boat with a single hull.

Multihull......................A boat with two or more hulls. *See Catamaran and Trimaran.*

Navigation Rules...............Universally recognized regulations for boats and large vessels to observe for safety when meeting underway, specifying which boat stands on and which gives way.

No-Go Zone.....................Roughly a 90° area that is too close to the wind for a boat to sail effectively.

Outhaul........................A piece of running rigging that pulls the clew of a sail to the end of the boom to stretch the foot of the sail.

Overtaking boat................Under Navigation Rules, the give-way boat that must alter course and/or speed when coming up on a slower boat.

Overtrimming...................Having a sail pulled in more than the optimum amount for the boat's point of sail.

PFD............................Personal flotation device, or life jacket, an essential piece of safety equipment aboard a boat.

Port...........................The left side of a boat when looking forward.

Port tack......................A boat's attitude when it is sailing with wind coming from the port side.

Port-tack boat.................Under Navigation Rules, the give-way boat that must alter course and/or speed when meeting a starboard-tack boat.

Powerboat......................Under Navigation Rules, a vessel under power is the give-way vessel when meeting a vessel under sail, except in the case of large vessels or ships, which cannot maneuver easily and should be avoided by sailboats.

Puff...........................A brief increase in wind velocity.

Range of tide..................The depth difference between high and low water.

"Ready about"..................The traditional command for "ready to tack."

"Ready to tack"................The command for preparing to change direction by turning through the wind.

Rudder.........................The movable fin attached to the stern that is used to steer the boat through its attachment to the tiller.

Run............................The downwind point of sailing approximately 150° to 180° off the wind, with the stern facing the wind and the sails between three-quarters and all the way out.

Running rigging................The movable pices of rigging used to set and operate sails, including halyards, sheets, cunninghams, boom vangs and outhauls.

Safety position................A way to take a break from active sailing, with the boat in a close-reach direction and the sails let all the way out to spill the wind.

Scoop recovery method..........A method of righting a capsized boat with the helmsman standing on the centerboard to pull the boat up while the crew holds onto a cockpit structure and gets scooped aboard as the boat comes upright.

Sheet..........................A control line for a sail, like the throttle, used to trim a sail in or out to adjust the angle at which the wind hits the sail.

"Sheet in".....................A command for pulling in a sheet to trim a sail.

"Sheet out"....................A command for letting out a sheet to trim a sail.

Shrouds........................Pieces of standing rigging that hold the mast from falling sideways.

Sideslipping .... Sideways, rather than forward, motion of the hull, prevented by the use of a centerboard, daggerboard, leeboard, or keel.

Spreader .... A short horizontal spar near the midpoint of the mast that spreads the shroud away from the mast to increase leverage and stability.

Square knot .... A pair of overhand knots that is useful for tying two lines together quickly and securely.

Stand-on vessel .... Under the Navigation Rules, the vessel that maintains course and speed.

Standing rigging .... A set of wires called shrouds and stays used to help the mast stand upright.

Starboard .... The right side of a boat when looking forward.

Starboard tack .... A boat's attitude when it is sailing with the wind coming from the starboard side.

Starboard-tack boat .... Under Navigation Rules, the boat that maintains course and speed when meeting a boat on port tack.

Stays .... Pieces of standing rigging that hold the mast from moving forward and back.

Stern .... The back end of any hull.

3 Ts .... Tiller toward trouble, the safety maneuver to steer away from hazards.

Tack .... The corner of a sail between the luff and the foot.

Tacking .... To change directions by turning the boat's bow through the wind. Like "hard to lee," tacking can be the helmsman's warning when putting the helm down to tack through the wind.

Telltales .... Pieces of yarn or cloth attached to the shrouds or stays to help show the flow of air and wind's direction.

Tender .... A small boat, usually propelled by oars or an engine.

Tide .... In bodies of water open to the ocean, the rise and fall of the water level on a predictable schedule due to gravitational pull.

Tiller .... The lever attached to the rudder to steer a boat.

Tiller extension .... A short lever hinged to the forward end of the tiller to enable the helmsman to steer while sitting farther forward and away from the tiller itself.

Trim .... The adjustment of sails in or out to find the optimum setting in relation to the wind direction and strength.

"Trim in" .... A command for pulling in a sheet to adjust a sail.

Trimaran .... A form of multihull boat with three hulls.

Trimtales .... Yarn or cloth attached to both sides of a sail near the luff to show the flow of air across the sail and allow the adjustment of the sail until they stream straight back to indicate the optimum trim.

Upwind .... The direction of movement toward the wind.

Upwind sailing .... Sailing in the direction of the wind, which includes close reaching and close-hauled sailing.

Vang .... *See Boom vang.*

Weather eye .... Attention to warning signs of changes in wind, tide or weather.

Windward .... The direction, in relation to the boat, from which the wind is blowing.

Windward boat .... Under Navigation Rules, the give-way boat that must change course and/or speed when meeting a leeward boat on the same tack.